Bicy͏ ͏nanics

Steve Snowling and Ken Evans

BICYCLE MECHANICS

in workshop and competition

 Springfield Books Limited

© 1986, 1989 Steve Snowling and Ken Evans

Published by Springfield Books Limited, Norman Road,
Denby Dale, Huddersfield HD8 8TH, West Yorkshire,
England

First edition 1986
Revised and reprinted in paperback 1989

Design: Douglas Martin
Photography: The photograph on p.43 is by kind
permission of Mike Dawson; all other photography is by
Graham Watson
Typesetting and origination: Jamesway Graphics,
Middleton, Manchester.
Printed and bound in England by The Bath Press

British Library Cataloguing in Publication Data
Snowling, Steve
    Bicycle mechanics: in workshop and competition.
    1. Bicycles. Maintenance & repair
    I. Title II. Evans, Ken, *1944–1987*
    629.28'772

    ISBN 0-947655-15-8

Cover pictures
front: The team mechanic coming to the rescue of
Sean Yates during the Tour de France
back: Steve Snowling at work in a makeshift
workshop during a six-day race

Contents

1 Introduction

A racing bike isn't cheap, and once you have bought one the expenses don't stop. You need two bikes at least, several sets of wheels and other spares.

A serious rider has to train every day. He has to spend money on travelling, eating well, looking after himself. For all this preparation and expense to be wasted by bad mechanics is a nonsense, not to mention frustrating. There is nothing more soul-destroying than training to a peak for a big event, only to find that your bike lets you down because it hasn't been correctly maintained.

So you must learn how to get the best from your bike: how to keep it in top condition even though it might be ridden every day. It makes practical sense, and financial sense too.

I was a racing cyclist, and still an amateur, when I started — almost by accident — to spend more and more time looking after bikes, rather than riding them. Now I am a professional mechanic, and still learning. I've written this book to pass on some of the lessons I have learned — some early on, others only recently — so that racing cyclists, and those who look after racing cyclists, can benefit from my experience.

It isn't a manual of basic mechanics. Every cyclist learns the basics, so I'll assume you already know them. But it isn't highly technical either. I've packed the pages with as much commonsense instruction as possible, together with some examples of how these lessons have helped me in my professional career.

A few people can have a full-time career in race mechanics, or work in one of the many specialist cycle shops to be found in every country. I certainly wouldn't try to discourage anyone who wanted to try to break into the "circuit" of pro mechanics; in fact, I would welcome the company.

It's a hard life, on the move all the time, and not being home much. But it is interesting and sometimes well-paid. However, you need to invest a lot of money first, to build up the necessary tools and tackle to be able to do your job well.

You don't get a lot of thanks, and you are out in all weathers. It is nice when the sun is shining, but there are a lot of cold, wet evenings too. Occasionally while I'm working late at night, one of the riders comes out with a cup of tea and a cake — and that makes a lot of difference!

We need more top mechanics to look after amateur teams at both domestic and international levels. There have been times when federations have been crying out for someone experienced to send overseas with teams, and the right candidates just haven't been there.

For being a top mechanic is a very specialised job. There is certainly no school for it, except that of learning by your own mistakes — yet another good reason for writing this book.

2 The tools of the trade

The home workshop

Working on bikes is a lot easier if you have the right place to work, equipped with the right kind of tools and storage.

First of all you need a stout work bench, preferably with cupboards and drawers below it, to keep everything as tidy as possible; and you need to have a good vice firmly attached to the bench. If you can also attach the work bench to the wall, it will then avoid all the rocking and swaying when you are working on something heavy or tough to move.

Another prerequisite is an abundant supply of clean rag; you can never have enough of it.

Neat and tidy — an indoor workshop.

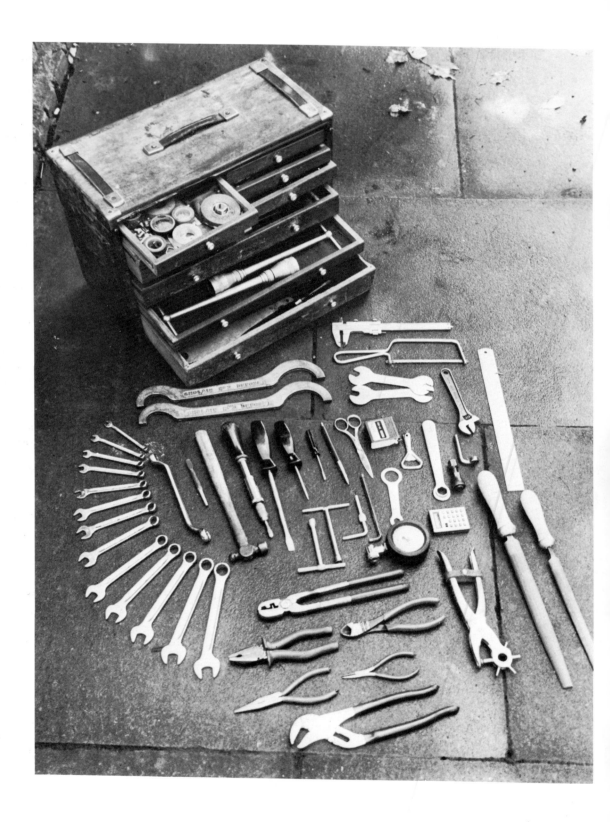

Basic tools — some cycle-specific, some general-purpose tools.

10

Basic tools

The following tools you should always have to hand (they are quite common and not specific to bike use, so are easy to find):

- ☐ A set of combination spanners (from 6 to 18 mm), open at one end and ringed at the other
- ☐ A set of allen keys: 2, 2.5, 3, 3.5, 4, 5, 6 and 7 mm to cover most needs
- ☐ Screwdrivers: a small one for adjusting gears, a medium and a large one, plus a medium cross-point one
- ☐ A pair of combination pliers
- ☐ A pair of cutters for spokes and cable
- ☐ A pair of long-point pliers for fiddly work, such as getting into brake levers
- ☐ A pair of fine cutters for cutting fuse wire, and for cutting away the tied and soldered joint if you have a spoke breakage on a track wheel
- ☐ A pair of slip-joint grips
- ☐ Two adjustable spanners: a 4-inch for odd-size nuts, and especially for realigning brake stirrups; and a 15-inch (the largest size that will fit in your box) to be used for general purposes
- ☐ A hacksaw
- ☐ A set of files: flat, half-round, round, square, and of different sizes
- ☐ A wire brush for cleaning out the files
- ☐ A two-speed electric drill, and a good drill set ranging in half-sizes from 2 to 13 mm
- ☐ A set of punches for marking out things that need to be drilled, and for pushing things out, like cables on brake levers
- ☐ A couple of hammers: a 4-ounce hammer (like a toffee hammer), and a 12–16-ounce hammer for heavier work
- ☐ A plastic hammer, for use on a frame or to straighten a chainring
- ☐ A 60-cm straight-edge — very useful for checking whether a saddle is level
- ☐ A measuring tape
- ☐ A 12-inch (30-cm) rule
- ☐ A 6-inch (15-cm) rule
- ☐ A Vernier caliper

(All measuring tools should be calibrated in inches and in metric units. Metric is becoming more popular now, but some imperial sizes remain.)

- ☐ A small pipe-cutter, for trimming off the ends of handlebars much more squarely than you can do with a hacksaw
- ☐ A leather punch — useful for crash-helmet straps
- ☐ Various taps and dies:
  - ☐ 3-mm tap for tapping out rear ends
  - ☐ 5-mm tap for bottle-cage braze-on bosses and gear-lever bosses
  - ☐ 6-mm tap for brake centre bolts and retapping stripped bottle-cage bosses
  - ☐ 8-mm tap for clearing out bottom-bracket axle threads
  - ☐ 10-mm tap with 1-mm-pitch thread for clearing out the gear hanger thread on a frame
  - ☐ 5-mm die to clean up various screws and the thread on a quick-release skewer
- ☐ Plus the appropriate tap wrenches and die stocks
- ☐ An adjustable reamer to cover between 22 mm and just over 27 mm, for cleaning out seat tubes and fork columns, plus the appropriate wrench
- ☐ A felt-tip pen
- ☐ A ball-point pen
- ☐ Various adhesive tapes and adhesives

Cycle-specific tools

The following necessary tools are specially made for cycling:

- ☐ Chain pliers for riveting and unriveting chains
- ☐ A set of freewheel removers to cover all sorts of blocks (Maillard, Regina, Campagnolo, Shimano, Sun Tour, etc.)
- ☐ Cone spanners
- ☐ Sprocket wrenches
- ☐ Special tools for brakes and pedal dust caps
- ☐ Crank extractors for 14- and 15-mm end bolts
- ☐ Pedal flywheels for checking pedals after a crash
- ☐ Headset and bracket spanners for adjustments
- ☐ A good nipple key that will hold the nipple on four sides, not just two
- ☐ Tyre levers

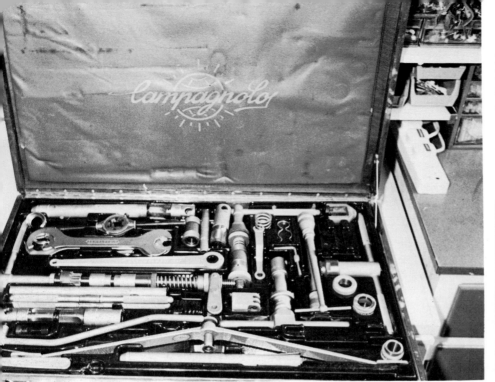

A Campagnolo tool set — a luxurious necessity.

A host of drawers of all sizes holds spares visibly and neatly.

Sheer luxury

A complete Campagnolo case of tools is ideal for frames, since it contains taps and dies for fitting and removing bottom bracket and headset, and for ensuring that all frame faces and threads are in line and square. It may seem like sheer luxury at first, but a Campagnolo tool case can become quite a necessity, above all when you first put a bike together on a new frame. And what's more, it's fun to use!

Keeping everything in order

It is essential that all the different components, spares and tools should be kept neat and tidy. Spokes, for example, can be kept in 12-inch lengths of square plastic down-pipe and stacked inside a cupboard. In this way they are kept together but separate. Then many items can be kept in small drawers of varying sizes. It not only helps to find things quickly, but it also looks tidy.

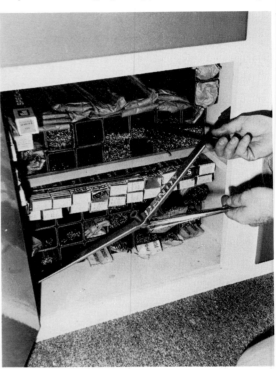

Spokes racked inside a cupboard, using lengths of plastic down-pipe to separate the sizes. The wheel dishing tool also fits into this cupboard.

Spares

Drawers and compartments are needed for the many spares which you should consider investing in, though the exact quantity will depend on how much work you are doing. You are always going to need things like:

- ☐ Brake blocks
- ☐ Brake clamp bolts and centre bolts
- ☐ Odd nuts and bolts
- ☐ Washers
- ☐ Bottle-cage bolts
- ☐ Seat-pillar bolts
- ☐ Extension-clamp bolts
- ☐ Expander bolts
- ☐ Gear rollers
- ☐ Ball-bearings (from 1/8- to 1/4-inch)
- ☐ Tub cement and brushes
- ☐ Spare sprockets and freewheel bodies
- ☐ Spare chainlinks (always keep the pieces left over from fitting new chains)
- ☐ Any other items which a bike-rider will break or use up

Stands

There are two basic types of bike-stand which you will find useful.

The first is a stand which holds the complete bike off the ground without the wheels needing to be fitted. This is an ideal stand for cleaning the bike, washing it and checking it, because the machine is held at the right kind of height. This type of stand looks bulky, but it collapses right down for transport. A wheel-jig can be fitted to it if required.

The other is a side-stand, which supports the left-hand seat stay and chain stay, holding the bike upright with the front wheel on the ground and the rear wheel clear of it (or not in at all). It is useful for running through gears, adjusting stems and bars, fitting handlebar tape and so on. You will find this type of stand at the trackside in six-day events, where it is used to keep the machine upright once the rider has dismounted, so that he can start again immediately.

The simple side-stand, which holds a bike by the rear stays, with the rear wheel just off the ground.

(bottom left) A collapsible workstand, which holds a complete bike with wheels clear of the ground.

(bottom centre) A close-up of the cradle and clamp, which together locate and secure the bicycle frame on the stand.

(bottom right) The same stand with a wheel-jig attachment instead of the frame clamp.

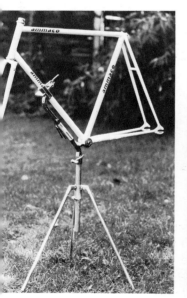

Have tools, will travel! Ready to go away on a race trip. The gear includes (left to right) tower cases, standard toolcase, hobby box, service toolbox, Campagnolo toolcase, buckets, spares, diesel can, compressor, workstands, and lots more.

Clothing

When I'm working I tend to wear bib-and-brace overalls, providing the weather isn't too hot. They are practical, hard-wearing and allow full freedom of movement. Your front is protected, and the back is higher than normal trousers or jeans. They are comfortable and have plenty of pockets.

In these pockets I always keep a nipple key for quick wheel adjustments. On the road I always have a pair of scissors in my chest pocket, plus a cone spanner for adjusting brakes. On the track I keep a Campagnolo 15-mm spanner in my back pocket for adjusting wheelnuts.

The travelling toolchest

When you go away on a race you need everything mentioned above with the exception of the work bench. All your tools should fit into boxes, and you will also need a portable vice which can be screwed to a suitable work top or table.

The best thing for carrying all the main tools is a wooden toolmaker's cabinet. I personally also carry a Campagnolo toolcase, plus two tower chests: boxes of 14 x 18 x 22 inches, which come apart into various sections by means of four turn-buckles. They can be variously adapted depending on how much stuff you need to take with you, or how much space is available.

Electrical kit, including an extension cable, and various kinds of fittings for many different countries.

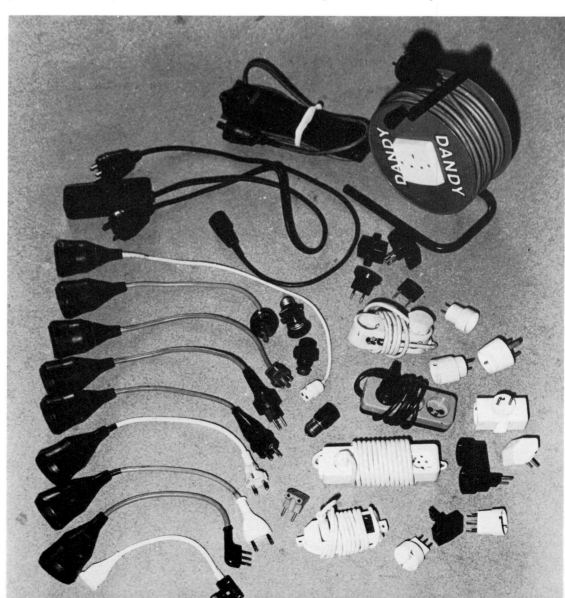

One box is designed to take a compressor so that it can travel safely, with a compartment above it for various electrical plugs, extension cables, a lamp, and a fan heater where necessary. Another box will contain spare parts, dishwashing liquid, oil, cement or shellac, rag in abundance, grease, a grease pistol, various chemicals for cleaning, latex cement for re-sticking tyre treads, white spirit for cleaning frame finishes, a small blowlamp for tying and soldering, and a roll of spokes of various lengths, enough to build a wheel from any given length.

Travelling spares

You should carry enough spares to be able to build up at least one spare bike and usually two. A typical "stock" for a race might include:
- ☐ Two sets of rear gears
- ☐ One clip-on front changer, and one for braze-on fitting
- ☐ A set of brakes complete with levers
- ☐ Spare brake centre bolts and lever rubbers
- ☐ Inner and outer cables
- ☐ Various lengths of handlebar stem
- ☐ A set of seat pillars, with diameters from 26.4 to 27.2 mm
- ☐ Two saddles
- ☐ Two sets of cranks, one of 170 mm, the other of 172.5 mm
- ☐ French-, English- and Italian-thread bottom brackets, with axles to go with them.
- ☐ One headset
- ☐ Two pairs of pedals, plus pedal axles
- ☐ A set of forks
- ☐ Several toeclips of different lengths
- ☐ Several pairs of toestraps
- ☐ Handlebar tape and plugs
- ☐ Two bottle cages
- ☐ Spare gear levers
- ☐ Seat bolts
- ☐ Ball-bearings
- ☐ Screws and nails for shoe-plates
- ☐ Several handlebars of different shapes and widths
- ☐ Several rims

The service toolbox

You will also need another toolbox which you keep separate from the main toolkit. This is the box you take with you in your service car or to the track centre. It means you don't have to keep transferring tools to a service case, and provides a reserve set of the important tools should anything go missing from your main box.

It should be a normal car-mechanic's case, and should contain: basic tools for fixing headset and bottom bracket, pedal spanners, allen keys combination spanners, screwdrivers, block removers, a spray-can of oil, and so on.

It can also include a pair of scissors, which you will need all the time to trim off bits of tape or solve other small problems. Once, for example, during a mountain climb in the rain, one of the riders complained that he couldn't breathe. It was the German Peter Becker, and the event was the Italian Tour of the Regions. He suddenly found his breathing getting harder. I had to cut his jersey down from under the arm while he was still riding.

I also have one long case about 14 x 6 x 32 inches. People usually think it carries a guitar, but it actually contains two workstands, a track pump, a vice, a shoe last and a wheel-jig, plus a special Campagnolo tool for fast and accurate saddle replacement.

See also the section on **The service vehicle** in Chapter 5.

Buckets galore

On a road event I would take six buckets with me — rectangular ones which fit inside each other. In the spaces between I put spare soap, brushes, a set of keys to open up water supplies where a tap is not fitted, a nail brush for cleaning up tape and getting into awkward corners, a cut-down water bottle, a medium brush for applying diesel to the chain, and a few padlocks for chaining up everything at night.

To help me stay sane and comfortable when I am cooped up in a six-day track event, or a succession of track events, I have what I call my

Packing up the "long case" containing workstands, track pump, vice, cobbler's last and wheel jig, plus saddle replacement tool.

Invaluable — a set of keys for opening up water supplies.

hobby box. This contains a Walkman radio and tape unit with headphones and speakers, a selection of tapes, an electric shaver, money and passport, a camera, a map, and an unbreakable thermos flask, plus tea, coffee, sugar, milk, a cup and washing gear. All this is kept in a weatherproof aluminium case, which goes with me everywhere. It is similar to a photocase, but made specifically to my own design, and lined with close-cell foam for safety.

The thing about luggage and tools is to buy exactly what you want and pay for it. Better to get the right thing once, and to have high-quality gear, rather than have to keep going back for replacements. If you need a specialised item, look hard for the right thing. Don't go for the nearest quickly available alternative.

For keeping you sane and happy — a "hobby box", with all life's little essentials.

3 Cleaning the bike

Setting up for cleaning a bike: two buckets, two brushes, a scouring sponge, and a container of diesel with a handy pot, plus a special brush to apply it with.

For a racing cyclist, it is important to establish a routine of cleaning the bike after every race. So you need to develop a logical cleaning routine, as indeed with every complex task connected with bicycle mechanics.

Always clean a bike before you attempt to overhaul it or do any other mechanical task. As a matter of form, try to keep your hands as clean as possible. This stops dirt and grease being transferred from one component to another. As you clean the bike, it often shows up problem areas which you can tackle when you start the overhaul.

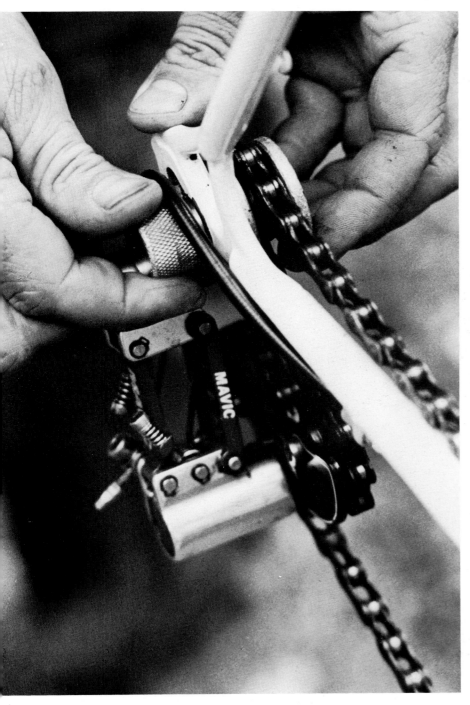

A "sleeping hub", which holds the chain in tension while the rear wheel is out.

Materials

The first thing is to assemble your cleaning materials. First you need two buckets of water, one of clear water, the other made very soapy with a mild liquid detergent. If the water is warm the soap works better, and the liquid evaporates a little and so dries more quickly too.

Then you need a pot filled with a 50/50 diesel-petrol mixture for cleaning the chain and the chainwheels. It also contains some oil, so the chain isn't left completely dry as with some other degreasing agents. And what's more, it is cheap and readily available. I personally carry the mixture around in a special petrol can, and tip the appropriate amount into my "pot", which consists of a cut-off feeding bottle.

You also need: two soft dustpan brushes, one for washing, the other for rinsing off; a double-sided pan scourer, with sponge on one side (for cleaning the tubes, handlebar tape and cable outers), and a scouring surface on the other (for cleaning the chain itself); and finally a softish brush for applying the diesel. It is worth putting a kink in the handle so that you can get in between the chainwheels and into other tricky places without the diesel dripping on to your hand all the time.

Cleaning procedure

The first step in cleaning the bike is to put it in the stand and take the wheels out. This allows you to get at a lot of normally inaccessible spots which the hubs or rims would normally cover, such as between the chain stays, underneath the brake bridges, behind the seat tube and so on.

To put some tension in the chain, use a "sleeping hub". (If you don't have one of these, a screwdriver between the drop-outs will do the job to some extent, but not as neatly.) This is so that the chain won't scratch the chain stay, and won't drop off the rings when you turn the pedals.

Always start your cleaning jobs by applying diesel to the chainrings, cleaning the outer ring first. As you clean the chainwheels, some of the diesel will already be getting on to the chain and loosening up some of the mess on it. It may also

A "modified" brush for applying diesel. The kink allows easier application between the chainrings.

be important to turn the cranks in their normal direction (i.e. clockwise), because some bottom-bracket sets (specially Campagnolo) have special threading inside the cups which tends to push dirt and water outwards providing the cranks are turning normally.

The next step is to clean the gear, turning the pedals again as you do it. Another good point about diesel is that when it gets into the gear rollers, as it invariably does, it doesn't dry out any of the lubricant in there. By this point the chain will have become quite well loaded with diesel, so when you come to wash it there won't be any

great problem with dirt.

Now treat the freewheel in the same way, but make sure you tip the wheel towards you as you clean, so that the diesel cannot drip on to the tyre and so damage or discolour it. At this stage you need only clean between the sprockets, not worrying about the internals of the freewheel.

The next stage is to take the scouring pad soaked in soapy water, and apply the soft, spongy side to the handlebars. Riders in long races tend to be handling bananas and spilling soft drinks, and as a result the bars and tape can get very sticky. The last thing a rider wants to feel the next

day is the left-over stickiness from the day before.

Most roadmen prefer the modern padded tape on the handlebars, which is easy to clean in the way described; but there are some who still use cloth tape, and for this you should apply the liquid detergent directly on to the tape, and use a couple of minutes' extra work with a nail brush. It comes up quite clean again.

With the same sponge you can clean all the bars, the stem, the brake levers, the cables (especially if they're light-coloured), and the front forks. Start this cleaning routine at the top of the bike, and gradually work downwards, so that some of the water drops down and starts to loosen up some of the grime on the parts below before you officially start to tackle them.

You needn't worry too much about the amount of soapy water splashing around. It won't hurt, providing you don't get it near the bottom bracket. Near the bracket, work from underneath. Some water might get into the cables; but again don't worry, because you will be checking these periodically; and if they show any signs of stiffness you will strip them out and re-grease them, or replace them if they're kinked.

Let the diesel find its way into and on to the gear rollers.

Tilt the wheel towards you as you clean the freewheel, to avoid diesel and dislodged grime dropping on to the tyre.

23

Use the soft side of the scouring sponge on the handlebars and tape.

You should use the soft side of the sponge on the main tubes, for which it is very convenient. But the hard-to-reach places should be attacked with a brush.

Now you have done all the areas which need to come up very clean, and thus kept the sponge clean for as long as possible. The time has come to use the rough side of the sponge for the chain, turning the cranks clockwise again so that it runs through the sponge held in your hand. Work on the top run of the chain (as in the picture), because that is the part which is under tension. Sponges don't last long under this type of treatment! But if the scourer lasts a stage race with six riders, then it's done a good job.

The strong soap solution takes care of the dust and grease picked up by the chain during a day's racing. Later on, give it another wash with clean water, and next morning give it a light oiling. This

Use the rough side of the scouring sponge to clean the chain by holding the top run of the chain and turning the pedals.

The soft brush comes in useful for cleaning awkward corners.

26

will stop it from rusting. And remember: the diesel will in any case ensure the chain won't go completely dry.

Still using the soapy water, go on to use one of the brushes to work on the less accessible areas, such as around the brakes, underneath the frame bridges, around the gear mechanism and behind the chainwheel. It's better than a sponge at this stage, because it lasts longer and doesn't catch on any sharp edges.

If you're handling a complete team of six riders, then you will need six full buckets with you, so that you won't have to break off the cleaning work part-way through to get more water. Use two buckets of soapy water to four buckets of clear water.

When cleaning the chainset and pedals, again make sure to turn them in the normal pedalling direction, because pedals too are often equipped with water-ejecting threads. The brush is very useful here for cleaning in between the crank arms.

The brush is great for the front changer too, taking off all the muck of the day's riding. If you don't clean your changer regularly it can get clogged up; the action loses its crispness, and it may not change just when you need it to. A daily wash avoids all this.

Incidentally, you can give the underside of the saddle some attention with the brush too. One rider in particular used to check for this. He used to look under the saddle, and if that was clean, then for him the whole bike had to be OK. If I know someone who has an idiosyncracy like that, then I try to pay attention to it, because it helps the relationship.

Lots of riders have their own little quirks. One might only worry about having his stem shiny,

The front changer is almost impossible to clean without using a brush.

*Why not give the underside of
the saddle a birthday?*

another about his handlebars being clean, while
another might concentrate on the part between
the cranks and the bottom-bracket cups. For
others, if the tape isn't clean, then they just don't
feel right. Tony Doyle, for example, would insist
on clean handlebar tape between every round of
the pursuit in world championships.

Typically, it takes around 15 minutes to clean a
bike, unless the day's conditions have been very
bad. But take as long as necessary to do the job
properly. As you do more and more, you will
speed up, and at the same time pay automatic
attention to detail. The way I clean the brakes, for
example, automatically cleans the brake blocks as
well. And if these aren't clean, you can't see any
foreign bodies sticking to them, which have to be
dug out to prevent bad braking or scratches on the
rims.

The next step is to clean the wheels. Here one of
the plastic buckets comes in handy again. Use it
to rest the wheel on. This gives you more height,

and allows a lot of the excess water to run back
into the bucket. Use the brush again: it's great for
cleaning the hub and between the freewheel
sprockets, which is where you should start. Don't
worry about water getting in the freewheel. It can
always be oiled later.

When you get to the rim, use the length of the
brush along the rim, not across it. In that way you
make the best use of the brush; and as you clean
the rim, so you also clean the tyre. Use a nail
brush to get off any stubborn marks, and always
use soapy water.

Once again, don't worry about water hurting
the tyre, even if it is a silk tyre. Water is a natural
aggressor, but in the circumstances you can do
little about it.

Clean the treads too. This helps take off the grit,
and gives you a good chance of spotting anything
sticking in the tyre which could later cause a
puncture.

Now put the wheels back on the bike again. Use

Clean the wheels, using the bucket to give you more height.

the rest of the soapy water to clean off your brush, the little pot for the diesel, and the rim of the diesel can, which will start to smell if you don't keep it clean.

The next step is rinsing off; and once again you start at the top of the bike, with the handlebars. Use a dabbing motion, which shakes a lot of water off the brush and rolls the soapy water away. When you are rinsing the wheels, rotate them as you do it.

You can use a hosepipe instead, if you wish, but then you have to be careful that the water pressure doesn't force water into the bearing areas. With the right technique you can use high-pressure hoses; and some professional teams are already using steam cleaners, which work at up to 80 atmospheres. They are extremely quick,

and invaluable when you are handling a team of bikes at a time.

If you are dealing with several bikes in one wash, then usually the first bike is dry by the time you finish cleaning the last one; so it is ready for checking. If you are only doing one bike, then dry it before you start the check.

Of course, you can spend a lot of extra time with a dry cloth, even polishing the spokes if you like; but chrome spokes come up well anyway when cleaned with a brush — until they start to deteriorate, which is usually after one or two seasons. Stainless steel, of course, lasts much longer.

Only after cleaning the bike thoroughly, in the way described above, should you start to check it over.

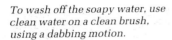

To wash off the soapy water, use clean water on a clean brush, using a dabbing motion.

4   The bike check

After every race you should check a bike systematically, concentrating on the most important areas of tyres, wheels, gears and brakes.

You must start with a clean bike, because then you can see what you're looking at. If a bike is covered with dirt you can miss cracks in the frame, in a crank, and so on. And of course it is much more pleasant to work with clean hands.

The brakes
The first step is to drop the wheels out: the front one completely out, the rear one only just out of the drop-outs, so you can get at the brake blocks to remove any grit or pieces of stone imbedded in them. Dig out any foreign bodies with something sharp, such as an engineer's scriber or an electrical screwdriver.

When checking a bike, you can drop the rear wheel just out of the fork-ends, which gives easier access to the brake blocks.

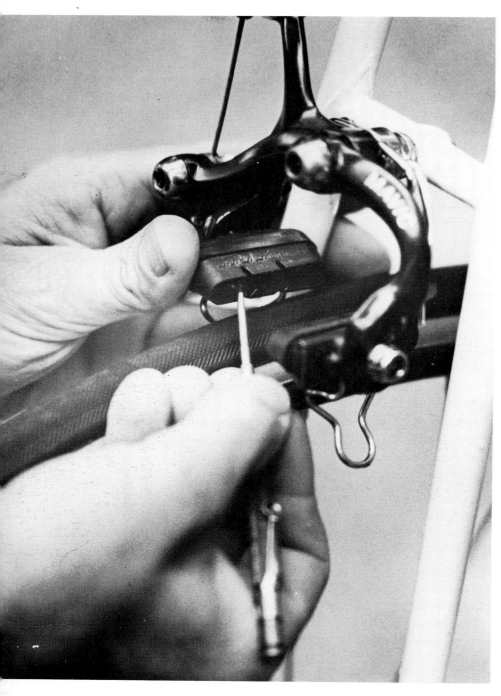

Use a sharp instrument to prise out grit or flints imbedded in the brake blocks.

Next, check for fraying cables at the brake lever, just where the cable enters the lever hood housing. Cables need to run freely, and any feeling of stiffness is a danger sign. It could be because the cable is snagged, or because one of the strands is broken, or simply because the weather has dried it out completely, in which case it needs to be changed. When you fit a new cable, don't neglect to put a ferrule on the bottom end, crimping it on with pliers. It looks neater, and stops the cable fraying.

Another problem is when a ferrule on the outer cable is squashed, and the cable is constricted as a result. The ferrule where the cable enters the lever is most important; the one at the stirrup end is not so vital. Cables often get damaged when a bike is leant over carelessly or put upside down, or as a result of a crash. A damaged ferrule can cause the cable to come in at a bad angle, and then it will fray. Crushed cable casing can produce stiffness in the cable pull, but trimming it back above the crush point may do the trick.

Make sure if you trim back the outer cable that you don't crush it again as you cut it. To avoid any such crushing, use a good tool such as a piano-wire cutter (which can also be used for cutting spokes).

The current type of Teflon-lined cable is good, and runs very smoothly, but it does need to be greased just like a normal cable. Any good-quality grease is fine for cables. Campagnolo grease comes packed in convenient tubs. If you have to grease any component, wipe your hands on a clean rag afterwards. I always have yards of it on a roll handy.

Check the other end of the cable too; and if any of it is kinked or fraying, don't be tempted to give it "just a bit longer". You cannot afford to have bad braking, and you will always find that if a cable snaps it will be at some critical moment.

One advantage of the new type of brake lever which allows the cable to run through the handlebars is that there is less chance of cable damage.

Brake adjustment

You don't usually have to adjust the brakes every day; but it can become necessary in extreme conditions, such as racing in the mountains or in rain, when quite a lot of rubber can be worn off the brake blocks. If a new cable has been fitted, then there will initially be an element of stretch, which means an adjustment at the end of the first day; but after that, the only adjustment needed will be as a result of brake-block wear.

I personally like to adjust the blocks so that the lever is about half-way to the handlebars when it is pulled tight; but this is a matter of taste, and some riders prefer a different adjustment. Sean Yates, for example, would always have his brakes adjusted so the levers came right up to the

This is a danger-point for cables to fray — just where the cable enters the top housing of the brake lever.

Crushed casing can cause stiffness in the cable run. A frequent place for such damage is just above the brake-lever ferrule.

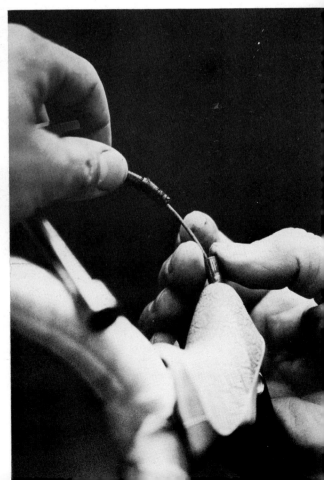

Adjusting the brakes using the stirrup adjuster.

A hypodermic oiler helps to lubricate the brake spring where it engages the lower end of the stirrup arm.

handlebars when he was doing an emergency stop. Whatever a mechanic did to his brakes, he would readjust them to the way he wanted.

Occasionally you will get squeaky brakes, and the remedy is a spot of oil on the brake spring where it notches into the stirrup arm. Also oil the bushing on the brake lever to which the cable is attached. For critical oiling like this, use a hypodermic needle filled with light oil.

Gear function

Checking the gears involves making sure that the mechanisms, both front and rear, don't cause the chain to overrun, either into the spokes or into the gap between freewheel and frame — and also ensuring that the gears work properly in all sprockets on both chainwheels.

Run the chain up and down the freewheel several times, moving the lever firmly but not

Checking the gear change.

Investigating cuts in tyre treads with a scriber.

Wheels and tyres

Tyres

It is vital to make sure that racing tyres are in good condition. So after each race, go round each tread looking for cuts, flints or bits of glass. Once again, use an engineer's scriber to investigate the cuts and see how bad they are.

If the cut is only to the depth of the rubber, then just fill the cut with rubber compound (or black Bostik works quite well). If the cut has penetrated the tyre carcass, then your tyre has to be changed. The idea of filling the cut is so that flints and glass can't work their way into it and cause a puncture. If you have to fill a cut, then do it with most of the air out of the tyre.

Naturally, if there is a bulge or a buckle in the tyre, this will already have shown up, probably even at the cleaning stage, and a new tyre will have to be fitted.

Wheels

There is no need to remove the wheels or put them in a trueing jig for basic checking. Simply use the distance from the brake block or your thumbnail, or sometimes both, to gauge the state of the rim.

If you find any buckles, you usually correct them by tightening spokes rather than by loosening them. Wheels tend to slacken themselves in use rather than tighten.

Often a rider will know there is a problem because he can feel it even in normal riding. If you can't see the flat spot, then you'll have to do the complete job and true it in a jig with the tyre off.

There comes a point when a rim must simply be scrapped. You can't use a rim on a racing bike if the rider can feel it bumping on flat roads or it is causing bad braking — though you might ride it on a hack bike.

Give the rims a basic check after every race; but if you have to change a tyre because of a puncture, this gives the opportunity for a thorough check and re-true in a jig.

Check the hub bearings for play by feeling for

forcefully, and watching to see that there is no "jumping".

You don't often encounter trouble with the levers or the gear cables, but in any case check that the cable runs smoothly, that it remains in tension, and that the operation of the lever is neither too easy nor too hard. Then tighten, loosen or change the cable as necessary.

Quick corrective treatment for a slightly buckled wheel — tightening spokes to correct them, rather than loosening them.

sideways movement at the rim, because any play at the hub will be magnified. A small amount of play is acceptable, but if the bearings are too tight you will not feel any play unless you check the cones themselves.

Test for play in the bottom bracket by rocking the cranks inwards and outwards. Any play will be magnified at the end of the crank.

The bottom bracket
Once again, any play in the bracket bearings is magnified by movement at the end of the cranks. Try rocking them sideways to check for play, and do this with the cranks in two or three different positions. Also, listen for any sound, which will indicate that the bracket either is dry or has water in it — and in both cases it will need to be stripped out. If you find some play with the cranks in one position and no play with them in another, then the odds are that there is some pitting of the cups.

Checking the hubs and bracket bearings need not be the subject of a daily check, but it should be done frequently.

Pedals, toeclips and straps
Check for bearing play and wear and adjust or replace as necessary. Check for wear and play between the shoe and the pedal on clipless pedals and that the release mechanism still offers adequate security. Check pedals fitted with clips and straps carefully. If a toeclip breaks during a race, this can be upsetting; if a strap breaks or gives during a sprint, it can cost a rider a victory. So don't leave these components out of your regular check.

The most common places for a toeclip to break are either across the fixing plate, where the screws bolt through, or in the tight bend around the toe.

Check that the toestrap buckle is still in good order, that it isn't badly rusted, that the rivet isn't about to break, and that the leather of the strap is still gripped by the serrations on the buckle. Try this in several positions.

Tightness
You obviously cannot go around checking that every nut and bolt is tight all over the bike, day in, day out. If it has been properly put together, a bike shouldn't shake nuts and bolts loose very often. So periodical checks are fine, in addition to thorough checks before major events.

Watch out for the bottle cage working loose. To tighten or check this, use a ball-ended allen screwdriver which allows you to get at the bolt from an angle of up to 30 degrees off centre. Then it is very quick to use, and good for awkward

The bend of the toeclip is a frequent site of a breakage, so check it regularly.

Also check that the toestrap buckle works properly.

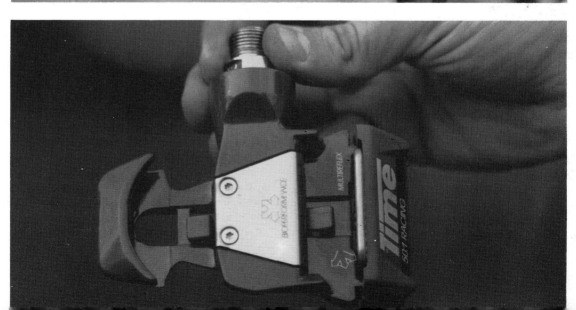

Clipless pedals require little or no maintenance.

positions such as when working from a service car.

You can't be casual about nuts and bolts being tight; on the other hand, you should be able to have confidence in your own work. On a stage race, check all the bikes for tightness before the event, with emphasis on the gear-hanger bolt, the crank and chainwheel fixing bolts, and the brake centre bolts. If you have put the bikes together yourself, then you know that everything will be tight.

Phantom squeaks

Sometimes a rider will tell you that something doesn't feel right on his bike, and that he can hear a squeak. This of course means making a special effort to track down the problem. You start with the freewheel itself, the hubs, and the bottom bracket, and eliminate as you go. Then it could be in the pedals; or maybe the pedals weren't greased when they were threaded into the cranks. After that, you start looking for cracks in the frame.

On the Peace Race, a rider told me he had a squeak coming from the front of his bike, and he feared that his forks were going to break. He changed bikes during the stage, and afterwards I tried to find the phantom squeak. I took the forks out and could find nothing; but when I took the headset apart, I found he had been forced to use Araldite to fit it into what was basically quite an old frame. The Araldite had lost its bond and was causing the creaking noise. It was quite harmless, but worrying at the time.

You always hope that the squeak won't turn out to be in the bottom bracket, because that is one of the more difficult jobs; so you try to eliminate any other possibilities first.

If you put another back wheel in and the squeak disappears, then look to the freewheel or the rear hub for the trouble. Then try oiling the gear rollers, check the pedals are greased, check the frame for cracks — and only then might you have to take the bracket apart.

Incidentally, about cracked frames — they aren't usually the result of a fall, but of metal fatigue. And if you keep the bike clean, then they are quickly spotted in the course of normal cleaning or drying. You will see a disturbance in the paintwork, a line of dirt, or even rust.

End of season

At the end of a hard season the temptation is to clean the bike and put it away for the winter. But if this is all you do, then you are wasting an opportunity. Far better to give the bike a basic overhaul before putting it away. This will give you time to get replacements for worn or damaged parts, and to make sure that there is no deterioration while the bike is in hibernation. You will thus save time at the start of the new season.

Fit a new chain, new brake blocks, new cables and handlebar tape. Look at the condition of the chainwheels, and check for play in the front and rear gears. Take a firm grip with your hands, and try to rock and twist the mechanisms to see if the rivets are worn. On the rear gear, twist the parallelogram; on the front changer, try to twist the cage.

If you feel movement with hardly any twisting effort, then you'll have to fit a new mechanism, and either scrap the old one or relegate it to a training bike. It may be that a gear will still change satisfactorily for training purposes, but lacks the positive change needed for racing.

Take a look at your saddle. Leather tops on foam-padded saddles can get worn, and any rough patches where the leather is going can give trouble and cause soreness in the long run; so in such cases it's best to consign them to the dustbin.

The winter bike needs special attention because of the weather it must endure.

Your winter bike needs to be just as sensibly dressed as its rider — so make sure you fit mudguards.

44

The winter bike

Although your winter bike need not be as well and regularly maintained as your racing machine, it needs certain special attention and special equipment to help it do its job well of carrying you safely through the winter's training.

You should have good mudguards for a start, and they should not be adjusted too close to the tyres. This allows you to ride through snow if necessary without the wheels clogging up. For safety's sake, spoke and pedal reflectors are worthwhile, and also a good set of lights.

The machine will need a lot of lubrication, because inevitably it won't get as much attention as your racing bike. It needs to be well lubricated in the hubs, bottom bracket and pedals, and requires regular oiling of the transmission, using motor oil rather than standard cycle oil.

Because the weather will be cold, use thicker handlebar tape to insulate the hands from the cold metal. Ride wider, heavier tyres. Tubulars can be used, but they should be tough enough to cope with all the gritting of the roads that winter brings. Tyre-savers can be an immense help with this.

Raise the bars a touch, and lower the saddle, because you will be wearing more layers of clothing against the saddle, and also around your neck. A lower position will help you to keep your head up. Otherwise, the position is similar to that on your racing machine.

One other change is to go over to Dunlop rim cement on the winter bike, rather than the Clement which is better for racing machines. This is because Dunlop remains tacky in cold weather and doesn't go brittle. If you have built up a base of Clement on your rims, then it is quite all right to put a layer of Dunlop on top. But it doesn't work the other way round.

5 Race service

The routine

Good race service is about being calm and staying that way. You have a couple of spare bikes on top of the car, a rackful of spare wheels, and two or three more inside the car with the quick-releases set ready. Inside the car you have tools, oil, sticky tape. There should be no reason to be nervous — though for myself I must admit that it does still get to me sometimes.

The first time I did race service I was certainly nervous, wondering what might go wrong. But I've found since that if you are well prepared you can usually handle any situation. And experienced riders will make your job easier.

Front-wheel changes can be done without the rider having to dismount.

Crashes demand coolness from the mechanic to sort out problems with minimum loss of time.

Open roads, on the other hand, make life a little more difficult, because you are effectively only able to use half the road. This makes for traffic jams, which in turn make it tougher and slower to get to your rider. And it can, of course, add to the hazards of driving past the field or past groups of riders.

The wheel-change

If a rider has a front-wheel puncture, all he has to do is to drop out the front wheel and hold the bike upright, preferably with both feet on the ground, while you put the new wheel in.

With a back-wheel problem, the rider should make sure he is in top gear on the freewheel (it doesn't matter which chainring), and undo the brake quick-release. This makes it much easier to get the wheel out. Experienced riders will not only have changed their rear mech into top gear, but often, if they have seen you a long way off, they will have got the punctured wheel out ready.

If you can't be sure which wheel is affected, grab a pair of wheels as you jump out of the car, just to make sure.

When you get to the bike, put the chain on to the smallest or next-smallest sprocket on the new wheel, and pull the wheel back into the frame. Check that the rider is keeping his bike upright, as this stops the chain coming off the chainring.

Once the wheel is in, and the rider is back in the saddle — though often there is no need to dismount — then you give him a push start while he gets his feet back into the clips and gets his gear rolling.

Crashes

When several riders fall, there is instant chaos. The road is blocked as all the team cars stop, and you could be a good way back in the column — too far to actually see the crash, and only able to hear it on the race radio.

Don't wait to find out if your riders are involved: just get out of the car, close the door, grab a pair of wheels and run to the scene. When you get there, look for your own riders, and do the

Getting the rider moving again after a puncture. The mechanic, carrying the punctured wheel, pushes the rider until he can get his gear turning.

You are often working on bikes or wheels on the roof rack while the car is moving.

best you can for them. This may mean just changing a wheel and pushing a rider off. However, it may be something worse, like a bent gear; and then you have to come back to the car, which is hopefully a bit closer by now, and grab a spare bike. Bent bars, bent saddles, and bent toeclips or bottle-cages, can be sorted out on the spot.

When you arrive at the scene of a crash, you naturally look for your own riders on the floor, but you should also look further up the road for other riders who might have stopped. Perhaps they have been involved in the crash but have got themselves underway again, only to find a

softening tyre, a wheel which is buckled or some other problem. Look off the road too, especially if you are on a raised piece of road, or if there are ditches on either side where riders might have been thrown.

In the Peace Race I once heard a voice crying out "Steve! Steve!" But I couldn't see anyone at first. Then I scrambled down an embankment where I thought the voice was coming from, and found a rider snarled up in some brambles. As it turned out this rider wasn't even in my team, but in such circumstances you have to help any rider.

Bike-changes

Normally, when you jump out of a car to give a service, you have only a pair of wheels with you. But sometimes a wheel isn't enough. You find that something has snapped, or a chainring is bent, a gear useless, a pedal smashed, or the frame is damaged beyond riding. Then you have to give a bike-change, and get the rider moving again.

Your next problem is to try to get his own bike repaired. If possible, try to do this while the bike is on the roof-rack, on the move, so you can quickly regain the race again. Otherwise, repair it by the roadside.

A well-equipped team car, carrying three spare bikes and plenty of wheels, all easily to hand.

A simple but effective home made tool for setting quick-release mechanisms to the right width.

and haring down mountains. The best models I have been in are the larger-engined Citroëns and Mercedes, which, although quite heavy, do the job very well.

You also need a back window that will wind down all the way, so that when the mechanic is leaning out of it, or sitting or standing on the sill, he is not resting on glass.

Inside the car you will need some spare wheels, and also some spare parts such as front and rear gear mechanisms, a saddle, some brake cable and brake blocks. The boot should contain a side-stand and a spare track pump, along with a collection of spare tyres and frame pumps for use if you have to leave a rider to his own devices. (See also the section on ·The service toolbox· in Chapter 2.)

You need a roof-rack that will hold a bike on each side, ready to ride, held on only by a quick-release clamp on the seat tube. The principle is to have racks that will allow a bike to go on and off with a minimum of fuss, with quick-release fittings rather than nuts and bolts and straps. Apart from at least two bikes, there should be room on top of the car for a rackful of wheels.

Because wheel-changes must be fast, it is helpful to set all the quick-releases to a standard, which is the compact seven-speed. Make sure that all the wheels will slip easily in and out of everybody's bike. If the frame is too tight, then manipulate it to suit.

The service vehicle

The best kind of service vehicle is a big, powerful car, like a sports container bus, with very good roadholding and handling characteristics. This is because the team driver has to do things that nobody would do in normal motoring: manoeuvring, making fast decisions, sprinting past bunches, weaving in and out of other cars,

Special hub-width tool

Not all hubs are the same width, and fork-ends vary in thickness from manufacturer to manufacturer. However, since most frames use Campagnolo ends, I have made up a tool which allows me to set hubs with just the right adjustment to slip straight into the ends. One end of it is for for front wheels, the other for rear ones.

Using this as a standard, I can set spare wheels in the service car as necessary. But I need to know who is using what kind of end, so I can make an alteration from this standard to suit. For example, when I was working with the 7-Eleven team, Eric Heiden had his own special frame built with ends

You can do a lot for a rider by working from the service car.

which were reinforced; and this meant that whenever I had to do a wheel-change for him, I had to give the quick-release skewer adjustment a couple of turns as I was running up to him.

Service from the car

You can do an amazing number of jobs on the move, hanging out of the window of the service car.

You can adjust front and rear gears while the rider is still going under his own steam and not actually hanging on to the car. Lean out so that your shoulder or back is behind the rider's saddle, and from that position you can get to most of the jobs at the back end of the bike.

On one occasion, I even refitted a brake block and shoe on the move. The rider had hit a brick on the road, which had damaged the rim so badly that it had knocked the block right out of the shoe. I had replaced the wheel and sent him on his way, and only then had he found that one of his brakes just wasn't working. Stopping again would have lost too much time, and there wasn't a spare bike to fit him, so we had to do the job on the run.

Because of the way I take the rider's weight on my back or shoulder, I can either use both hands to work, or else use one hand to steady the bike and the other to work. I'm not exactly holding him, and he can get free in a moment if he wants.

You can adjust saddle height or gear levers fairly easily. But more difficult to do from the car are jobs involving the handlebars or adjusting the front brake, since these affect the steering. In such cases it is better to give the rider the tool and let him do the job for himself.

Commissaires tend to be pretty understanding when you have to do jobs like this, even if the rider has to hang on to the car while you are making the repair or adjustment. But they won't, for instance, allow it during a climb, when the rider would be getting some real assistance from the car.

The car driver

When performing such tasks you must rely on the skill of the team car driver — usually the manager — to give you the best chance of doing a good and

A mechanic tightens a slipping saddle without the rider having to dismount. The rider just holds on to the car while the trouble is tackled. Note how the mechanic uses his shoulder to steady the rider while he works.

quick job. He has to allow enough room for you and the rider between the car and the edge of the road, and he mustn't brake or accelerate too hard. And when, for example, you are climbing out of a window to get an extra wheel off the roof, you have to be sure that he isn't likely to skim you against a roadside wall.

The riders have to know that the car can stop as quickly as necessary to do a wheel-change. And the mechanic has to be sure that the driver will stop in a position which lets him get out of the car easily. Sometimes this isn't possible when there are two files of cars and the roads are narrow.

There have been times when I've had to jump out of the car straight into a ditch, run along the ditch and climb out further down to get to the rider.

Ideally, as the car is stopping, you are watching for where you are going to hit the road, avoiding big holes or rocks. Sometimes I will actually jump out of the car before it has stopped, hanging on to the door frame so that it starts me running, giving me speed to start with. I let go of the frame and push the door closed at the same time.

The stage-race mechanic

Servicing a bike at home, or in the comfort of a workshop, is the uncomplicated end of a race mechanic's task. The opposite end of the scale is probably the stage race, where the end of each day brings new problems with a new location.

To answer this particular challenge you have to be methodical yet flexible. And if you can do with less sleep than the next man, that helps a lot. It always means a very long day and a short night. You are often working before breakfast, and usually well after the riders have gone to bed and the other team officials have finished for the day.

During the day, even though you are in a car travelling behind the race, you can't really relax, because you always have to be on the alert for punctures and crashes. But the main part of your work comes after each day, when you reach the hotel, possibly after a long road journey from the stage finish.

Normally you have to travel from the stage finish to the hotel or overnight quarters, which first means getting the riders into the team vehicles and getting the bikes loaded. You do that as quickly as you can, bearing in mind that there are always riders wanting to tell you their life story, wander about, and take a long time getting into dry clothes. Part of your job when you get to the finish is to make sure that the bags are there for riders to get their dry clothes easily.

Loading the bikes is best and easiest if you have enough roof racks to take the bikes complete, or just with the front wheels removed, held on by the quick-release. Otherwise, you have to pack them into the vans or cars as best you can — either head-to-foot with the wheels in, or all the same way with the wheels out — packed so that they can't move about and get scratched in transit.

Hotel routine

When you arrive at the hotel, and even before you take the bikes off the roof, your first job is to find out where you are going to work. It could be anywhere, perhaps a mile away. You go there and assess the situation, hoping for covered, safe storage, preferably with a light — though if not you can use your own light provided power is available. There also needs to be water. If there isn't a place already set up, then you ask for one, or go out and find one for yourself.

You have to cope with all sorts of surroundings. In the Italian Giro delle Regione we had to stay in a nunnery, and our workshop was their enormous cookhouse. There was a giant cauldron on a fireplace, with steaks cooking next to it, and we had to work on the bikes in a cloud of smoke. Schools and barrack blocks are also common.

You even get used to working outside in bad weather. You wear waterproofs in the rain, and it helps you to wash off the bikes. But it's a different matter when you have to do jobs like sticking on tyres or stripping something down. At such times you need to be dry, and then you have to find a place that's under cover.

It's all the same to me if I work in the street outside a hotel, and on one occasion during the Giro d'Italia, that was just what I did. It was outside a very expensive hotel where they had told me they had no place for me to work — no water, nothing. So I asked the first porter I saw where the toilets were, walked in, filled up my buckets, walked through reception complete with bucketfuls of water, and set up shop right outside the main entrance. I washed and cleaned all the bikes, drawing quite a crowd; and afterwards the bikes went up into the hotel rooms. It was the only answer, because the hotel had laid on nothing.

It's always worth taking six buckets with you. Then, if you fill them all up first, you can do all the work on the bikes without having to leave them untended while you go for a refill.

Here is a brief summary of the routine, which is covered in more detail in Chapters 3 and 4. Put the first bike on the stand and remove the wheels. Then clean the chain, wash the whole bike, put the wheels back in, rinse the whole bike, put it aside, and continue with the next bike until the whole "team" of bikes is done. By that time the first bike should be nearly dry. With a clean rag, dry off any excess water and wipe away any dirt you have missed.

Check the brakes for adjustment; check the cables for fraying; make sure the gears work;

A team car forces its way up the outside of the bunch, horn blasting, to support a rider in a breakaway group.

check for play in the bottom bracket or pedals; check toestraps and clips. Check tyres very thoroughly for damage, cuts or flints; true up the wheels if necessary; check for bumps in the rims. Take the bike out of the stand and check the headset for play or pitting. This is quite a complete check, although it may not sound much.

After repairing or replacing parts as necessary, stack all the bikes together and chain them up for the night. Leave any oiling or greasing for the morning, together with any inflation of tyres.

Often there will be gear ratios to change as well, because of different terrain to come. This may be a decision from the team manager or team captain, or just an individual rider's preference. If you are unsure, you can often ask a mechanic from the country concerned, who is likely to know the terrain. And you can usually rely on a straight answer from another pro mechanic. If you're worried, you can always double-check on the gears he has fitted on his own team's bikes, just before you go to bed. There will be variations, too, depending on how each rider is going or on his riding style. As a last resort you can look at the profile map in the race manual, but it isn't always to be trusted.

Crashes often knock the stuffing out of a determined rider. The mechanic must help to bolster morale as well as getting the bike ready again.

Crisis management

You can get as many crashes in professional fields as during amateur events, and the riders can get just as nervous, whatever the licence says they are. So a mechanic has to be diplomatic, assess the difficult situation, and try to handle it in the best way possible.

On one occasion there was a big pile-up, and two members of my team, the Royal-Wrangler team, were in it. Both needed new front wheels. So instead of fitting up one rider and sending him on his way, I handed him the one front wheel I had brought and let him get on with it, while I sprinted back to the car for another front wheel. That meant that both riders could get away together, share the effort of the chase, and regain the main field — which is just what they did.

When someone crashes or punctures at a bad time, you should try to keep him cool by taking his mind off his immediate problem. Give him something to do: get him to hold the bike upright, and tell him to undo his quick-release and move the gear lever into top so that the rear wheel goes in more quickly. Give him a chance to get his breath back, and tell him his shoelace looks undone. It takes some of your concentration away, but it stops the rider panicking.

Panic is your enemy. In stage races and in big one-day events, you can find yourself sticking on tyres in the team car while it is descending a mountain pass, or even rebuilding a bike. I once had to strip a bottom bracket out just before a race start. I had 20 minutes to do the whole job, and thankfully everything went as it should.

Part of a team

If you are working with a team, you have an official function which extends beyond looking after the bikes. You are part of a team of officials, which has to be seen as a group working together. The mechanic's role is one of building and maintaining confidence. Above all you should stay cool and calm.

In a way, the officials on a stage-race team are like parents, giving the riders support and something to lean on. Once away from their home environment, riders can become unsure of themselves, and need this kind of support. Just being able to talk to a mechanic who is obviously calm helps them to be calm too — and this helps the team.

Individual tastes

I've worked with all sorts of riders, from the no-hopers to world champions like Britain's Tony Doyle or Denmark's Hans-Henrik Oersted. They all have their different temperaments, preferences and idiosyncracies.

I always found Oersted, for example, a perfect gentleman: extremely nice, and very approachable if ever you wanted help or advice. He liked his bike to be polished and sparkling 24 hours a day, which is very much as he tends to look himself! He always kept changing his position; even when he went training he took a spare seat bolt in case it broke while he was adjusting it. Once he even changed his saddle height during the final hour of the last Madison in a six-day.

The pressure of racing sometimes makes riders ask for changes which either are virtually impossible or you know will be wrong for them. So you make out you've done it, and the rider goes away happy.

It's usually gears and position that come in for such requests. Certain seat pillars, and certain handlebar extensions, are adjustable only to click-positions, and nothing in between is possible. So the rider has to have either his current position, or a considerably different one which you know would be wrong. Or perhaps you know that when you move the position, there may be something that you can't get as tight as before. So the tendency is to leave it.

There are other times when you know darned well that the gear is adjusted correctly, and that if you change the adjustment the chain will end up getting thrown off or down on to the bracket shell. Such requests are usually the result of nerves on the rider's part. So you tell a white lie and the rider is happy — and sometimes he even comes back afterwards and tells you how much better the position was, or how well the gear changed!

Every rider has his personal quirks. Danny Clark, for instance, uses steel bars in an alloy stem, and he always likes them left a little bit loose so that he can adjust them during the race. I didn't know at the time, so I automatically tightened the bars when I checked his bike and found them loose. As a result, when he came to adjust his position, he found he couldn't budge them!

One rider, a German called Uli Rottler, always got nervous before the start, and was always calling to have his brakes adjusted. So I got used to carrying the right spanner with me all the time, so that I could do the job without delay — although there really wasn't anything to do. It got so bad that his team-mates knew about it, and started to refer to that spanner as the Rottler spanner. Rottler isn't in the team any more — he is now a successful mountain bike rider — but the German riders still call the spanner after him.

This personal element means a lot to me. I'm not just working on bikes, but on bikes belonging to individual riders — an extension of their personality and their performance. I'm doing a service for them as much as for the bikes. So from time to time I get really upset or pleased when riders do badly or succeed. I remember how pleased I felt when Tony Doyle won his first six-day race, and with Danny Clark at the 1983 Berlin Six. Strange to say, I wasn't all that worked up when he won the world pursuit title. I suppose I had been calming myself down so much in between rounds of the pursuit that I wasn't then

capable of getting excited when it was all over. I had just done the job I was there for.

Changing a rider's position

A professional mechanic, having worked with so many different bike riders and on so many different kinds of racing, can often be in a position to offer helpful advice on a rider's position.

You will, of course, be familiar with the standard way of finding the classic road position, starting with the heel on the pedal. But this is only a guide, and may change depending on the type of event. A criterium position, for example, is closer to the track position than to a road position, with the bodyweight further forward.

If during a race you feel that a rider's position may be wrong, or that his weight distribution could be better, you should mention it to the team manager, who may then either discuss it with the rider, or in some cases simply tell you to make the necessary changes.

I once fitted a longer stem for a particularly tall rider, Remig Stumpf — a 14-cm instead of a 13-cm. He didn't notice the change at all as such, but did remark how well he felt that day.

With a stage-race or road-racing position, more weight tends to go on the back wheel, with less strain on the rider's arms. For criteriums, the relative positions of seat, pedals and bars don't change, but the whole body is rotated forward. Imagine the effect if you fitted a smaller front wheel, and you will get the idea.

6 The main bearings

If you are to look after any racing bike properly, you will have to know the correct way to remove and refit the bearings in the frame: the bottom bracket and the headset. Both main bearings require a similar operation, which involves setting the bearings so that there is minimum resistance and virtually zero play.

The bottom bracket

When you are dealing with a cotterless bottom-bracket set, make sure that you always use the correct removal tool. This is no time to try and botch the job, since a lot of damage can be done if a badly-fitting tool slips.

Start by using the correct socket spanner to remove the axle end bolt. And don't forget that it will have a washer too, which might not come out automatically as the bolt unscrews. The washer might even be made virtually invisible through grease. On no account leave the washer in place, otherwise you will probably strip the crank thread.

The extractor only needs to lock up in the crank, and it doesn't need to be terribly tight. Wind in the extractor and the crank should come off cleanly. The tapered part of the axle over which the crank fits should be perfectly clean and dry — no grease, no oil, just dry! This is the only metal-to-metal point on the bike which should definitely not be lubricated.

Clean everything as you go. Once you have removed the crank (it doesn't matter which one you start with), run a clean rag through the spline for the axle. If you grease the axle taper, then there is a chance that it will allow you to force the crank

Locking up the extractor tool in the crank. It does not need to be inserted with any great force.

Run a clean rag through the axle spline.

Using the correct peg spanner to undo the adjusting cup of the bottom bracket.

When a bracket cup is removed, the ball retainer usually comes out with it.

on too far, with consequent damage and a possible crank fracture at the axle spline.

Once you have removed both cranks, start to remove the locking ring of the adjusting cup, unscrewing anticlockwise since it has a right-handed thread. This then enables you to undo the adjusting cup itself, which also has a right-handed thread. Once again, use the peg spanner made for the bracket concerned.

The ball retainer usually comes out with the cup, and the axle can then be removed, cleaned with rag and examined. Check the bearing surfaces on the axle for pitting, and assess the amount of wear. There will be wear, of course, but the wear should be even, so that all you see is an even, shiny track. Check also for cracks in the axle, which can happen anywhere on the axle but are thankfully very rare.

Then out comes the plastic liner, for cleaning and refitment or replacement.

Incidentally, if you are taking out your bottom-bracket set for a respray, take the trouble to clean and separate all the parts at this stage. Don't just throw them all into a plastic bag, or you will later have the demoralising task of sorting them out again — all grease and rust — before

65

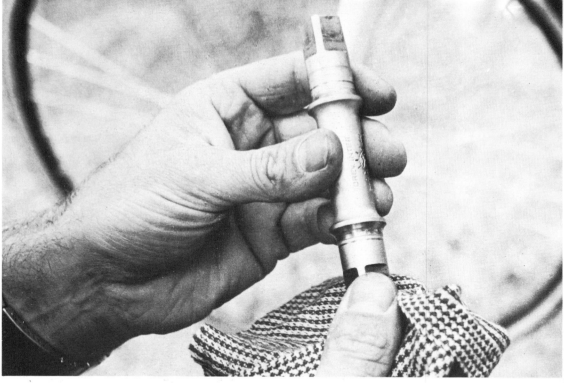

Look at the axle bearing surfaces for signs of pitting. Any wear should be even.

Removal of the fixed cup, again using the correct tool.

Check for wear on the bearing surfaces of the bracket cups.

Using a grease gun makes it easier to lubricate the bracket cup in just the way you want.

putting them into your refurbished frame.

I prefer to use clean rag (in huge amounts) for cleaning such parts, rather than a degreasing agent like paraffin or petrol or gunk, which has to be washed off with water afterwards anyway.

The final stage of the stripping down process comes with the removal of the fixed cup and its accompanying ball retainer. British and American threads, being left-handed, unscrew clockwise; French and Italian threads are right-handed so unscrew anticlockwise. With both bearing cups you check for wear and pitting, just as with the axle bearing surfaces. Pitting always tends to be worse on the right-hand side of the bracket (i.e. on the fixed cup), because it takes in more water.

You should change appropriate bearing parts

according to wear, and this depends on usage. For example, Tony Doyle, who is quite hard on equipment, would normally be into his third bracket set by the end of a road season.

Now that the bottom bracket shell is empty, take the opportunity to clean it out, again with rag.

After a respray, you may find that the bottom bracket threads are clogged with paint, so it is wise to put a tap through to clean them out before proceeding to refit the bracket set or to fit a new one. If you do put a tap through, clean out the

shell with a stiff brush, such as a bottle brush. The correct bottom bracket taps come as part of a facing tool, also used in frame-building, which ensures that the two faces of the shell are parallel. A top-class mechanic will never leave this kind of thing to chance, and will always have this expensive tool in his workshop, using it after a respray, and even with new frames, since often the finishing is not up to standard.

Now begin the process again, but in reverse. Grease the fixed cup using high-quality grease. It's best to use a grease gun, which makes the job

Screw in, finger-tight, the adjusting cup loaded with balls and grease.

cleaner and puts the grease just where it is needed. Grease liberally on to the ball track.

I often use loose balls in the cups, rather than ball races, whose cages have been known to bind up. Loose balls are a little trickier to put in. They are almost always quarter-inch balls, 11 per side. Don't follow the old wives' tale of leaving one out. If you are using loose ball-bearings, it is a good principle never to mix batches: better to discard the end of a packet than risk a mismatch.

Put a drop of grease on the cup threads (which makes greasing the shell unnecessary), and fit the cup (anticlockwise for British threads, clockwise for French and Italian), making sure it is very tight. Then refit the plastic liner and insert the axle, having first greased both ball tracks. Make sure that the longer taper of the axle is on the right-hand (chainwheel) side.

Now do the same with the adjusting cup, already loaded with balls and greased, screwing it in clockwise, finger-tight, before using a spanner.

With a bottom bracket axle there must be absolutely no play on the axle, and even a little resistance is acceptable. The sort of loading the bracket gets when a rider is putting his weight on the pedals means it is far better to have a slight amount of pre-loading on the bearings, rather than play, which would only be magnified under effort.

Bear in mind also that the resistance felt before you tighten the lockring will not be maintained, because tightening the lockring has the effect of backing off the adjusting cup on the threads, even though you hold it in position with one spanner while tightening the lockring with another. When you have finished, the axle will run smoothly, but you will be able to feel just the slightest resistance.

Now replace the cranks, making sure once again that there is no grease on the axle taper or the crank spline, but putting some grease on the axle end bolt. It makes no difference which crank

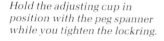

Hold the adjusting cup in position with the peg spanner while you tighten the lockring.

Firmly tighten the axle end bolts, using the crank arms and spanner as opposition levers.

you fit first. Do the cranks up very firmly indeed, using the correct spanner, and using the crank and the spanner arm as levers in opposing directions. Fitted this way, the cranks will not come undone again.

The final step, once the chainset is installed again, is to check that the front changer is still operating properly, because there might now be a slight difference in the chainwheel position relative to the changer if the right-hand crank has been fitted further on to the axle or not quite so far.

The headset
First take out the front wheel, and put a piece of tape around the handlebar stem where it enters the headset. This ensures you can replace it in the same position later. Slacken the allen key of the expander bolt, and loosen the wedge by tapping the bolt head with a light hammer.

When you remove the stem, you will probably be surprised by the unsightly state of the hidden section of the stem; but this is normal — the result of interaction between the alloy of the stem and the untreated metal on the inside of the head tube. Don't bother to disconnect anything else. Just turn the handlebars parallel to the top tube and hook

Tap the expander bolt head with a light hammer.

When tackling a headset, you've no need to undo brake cables or otherwise dismantle the handlebar assembly. Just hook the whole lot over the top tube.

Use one spanner working against another to free the headset locknut.

them over, so the whole handlebar assembly is out of harm's way.

Now use two spanners, working one against the other, to free the headset locknut. If you are intending to remove the headset components from the head tube, then you will also have to remove the front brake stirrup. Slip it over the handlebar and secure it with the quick-release.

The lower ball race and the crown race get the worst of treatment, with the vibration through the forks and the muck which is thrown up from the road. You can only inspect these by dismantling

the headset further, unscrewing the adjusting race and removing the accompanying ball race. As you unscrew this race, support the forks until they are freed.

The process is very much the same as with the bottom-bracket set. Remove each part, clean it and inspect it for wear. If you decide to carry on using a headset on which a race is slightly pitted, the pitting effect will be halted if you take it completely apart and reassemble it, because then the pitting surfaces will no longer coincide.

Don't forget to clean and inspect the crown

*If you intend to remove the
headset components from the
head tube and forks, you will
have to remove the front brake
stirrup. Again, don't undo the
cable; just clip it to the
handlebars, using the
quick-release.*

There are special tools for removing the frame races (left) and crown race (right).

race, and the upper and lower frame races. There are special tools for removing them from the frame without damage.

Incidentally, you have to do an extra checking job after a crash in which the frame or the forks might have been damaged. You need to check that the fork blades are in line again. Use a fork alignment tool, which will put them right again if they are not aligned. And while the forks are out, use a crown race cutter to check that the faces on top of the fork crown are still at right angles to the fork column. If they aren't, use the cutter to reface them. For even a minimal misalignment of the fork crown with the steering column can be enough to cause unequal wear and mess up a good headset.

Reassemble after cleaning, fitting new parts as necessary, and using a grease gun to grease the races and the balls. If any components are rusty, change them, because that means water has been in there for some time. You should also swap the ball races over to change any wear pattern. And always give an extra coat of grease to the lower ball race, because of the extra weather protection it will need.

Don't forget to lubricate the threads on the fork column: this is vital if you are using an alloy headset. Insert the fork so that the crown race is in position, and gradually screw down the adjusting race by hand. This is fairly simple if you are using ball races, but if you choose loose balls you must hold the adjusting race firmly down on the balls

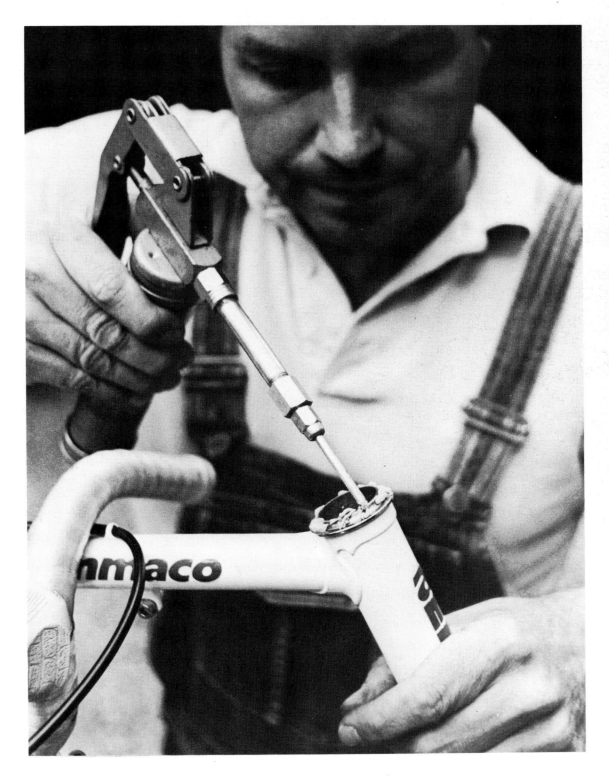

Grease races and balls on reassembly.

When reassembling, hold the forks so that the crown race is in position, and screw down the adjusting race by hand.

as it screws on to the column, to ensure that they don't go all over the place.

Once the headset is fitted finger-tight, you must refit the handlebar assembly before the headset can be adjusted, because the very action of the expander wedge tends to compress the headset.

So grease the expander wedge and the threads of the expander bolt, but don't grease the part of the wedge which comes in contact with the inside of the steering column, because it has to grip firmly. Grease the stem so it slides easily down

When you replace the handlebar assembly, don't tighten the expander, and leave the bars markedly off centre as a reminder that this job still has to be completed.

brake and tighten up.

Now comes the final headset adjustment. With the bike on the ground and the front wheel between your knees, you can test more easily for play and freedom of movement. Set the adjusting race by hand so that there is just a touch of play. This will disappear when you lock down the locknut, working in exactly the opposite way to the lockring on the adjusting cup of the bottom-bracket set. Tightening the locknut pushes the adjusting race further down.

With the front brake locked up and centred, you can apply an extra-sensitive test for play. Remove any excess grease, and the job is done.

The final headset adjustment —
best carried out with the front
wheel on the ground. Again, one
spanner is used to hold or alter
the adjustment, while the other
spanner governs the locknut.

into the steering column and will not corrode into it, and then fit it to the correct height, using the tape strip as a guide. Don't tighten the expander fully at this stage, and deliberately leave the handlebars off centre to remind yourself that you still have some adjustment to do.

Refit the front brake, but again loosely and clearly off centre, because you cannot centre the brake until the front wheel is inserted. Now put in the front wheel, take the bike out of the stand and set it on the ground. Centre the handlebars and

7 Frame problems

The two-piece fork-alignment checking and correction tool. When the fork ends are parallel, the two faces of the tool will meet exactly. The longer ends of the tool are used as levers to correct misalignment.

Using a length of twine and the alignment tool to check if the frame is in track. With the twine ends held taut, the twine should pass an equal distance either side of the seat tube, which can be measured with a rule.

If a frame isn't straight, whether through bad building or as a result of a crash, then it can cause problems. If the fork ends aren't parallel, then wheel spindles can become bent and eventually break. Gears don't work properly either, because the gear will always be out of line in relation to the sprockets.

If a rider has crashed, always check the frame alignment. Other danger signs are if spindles are bent, if the wheels simply won't go in and out easily, or if the quick-release isn't positive enough. You can often see a problem by driving along behind a rider. Then misalignment can be quite visible, because his wheels don't seem to be in line.

Checking for alignment

If you want to check or realign fork ends, you need a two-piece Campagnolo or similar tool for the purpose. The two parts of the tool should face together perfectly when screwed into properly-aligned fork ends. If they aren't aligned, the faces are clearly not in line either, and the ends of the tool can be used as levers to correct the situation.

Once you have established that the ends are parallel, the next thing is to check whether the forks are lined up with the head tube. This is done by putting a good wheel in to see if it is central on the fork crown. Try putting the wheel in the opposite way round to make sure. If you find the forks aren't aligned, then you must take them out and straighten them in a fork jig.

I have had a lot to do with frames, and the stiffest frame I ever came across was a Colnago belonging to Horst Schutz. But generally speaking, British Raleigh frames stand comparison with other European equivalents. Raleighs compare well with Colnago frames for looks and rigidity, and are often lighter.

There are a lot of superb small frame-builders around, and it is a pity that some of them are persuaded by their customers to build "Mickey Mouse" designs. You can make a modern frame, but it still has to be ridable, and steer well not just on the straight but also round corners. It has to be

in line and accurate, and finished off so that the components can be mounted without the threads having to be tapped out again.

Checking the track

Checking the track of the frame — that the main tubes are in line — is done using the fork-end alignment tool and a long piece of twine. You should do this when a frame doesn't look right from behind, or if the rider complains that it veers off to one side when ridden no-handed. It is also one of the checks you should apply after a crash, along with that of end alignment, cranks and pedals.

With the alignment tool in place in the rear ends, loop the twine around the head tube and pull each end tight at the outside of the rear fork ends. Then measure the distance from the string to the seat tube, which should be the same either side.

Sometimes the gear hanger can get bent, and this can be checked, again using a Campagnolo or comparable tool, with a wheel known to be true pushed right back in the drop-outs. Screw the tool into the hanger, and its extremity will fall near the rim. The tool rotates in the hanger, so you can compare the distance from the rim at various points, and any misalignment will be magnified so much that measurement is really unnecessary.

Rear-end width

It saves a lot of problems later on if your frame is built to take the kind of wheel you expect to use. This may sound simple enough, but you would be surprised at the number of frames that have to be adapted because the wheels won't go in cleanly — and that's not because the rear ends are out of line.

So it is best to decide what width of freewheel you are going to use before the frame is built. For roadmen I would suggest that the rear ends are spaced to take a seven-speed compact freewheel, which at 127 mm is a millimetre wider than a standard six-speed. For time triallists a standard six-speed is probably better, because they are unlikely to need seven sprockets, yet they will

Checking for a bent gear hanger, using another alignment tool. If the hanger is properly aligned, then as the tool is rotated, it will stay the same distance from the rim.

probably need to use a 12-sprocket at some time, and that isn't available in a five-speed. If in doubt, you can take a wheel along to the frame-builder, who will measure it to give you a perfect fit.

ends have been pulled outwards, they will no longer be parallel to each other. So you have to use the Campagnolo or similar fork-end alignment tools to correct that.

"Springing" a frame

This is something you will have to do frequently, usually with frames built to take a five-speed where the rider is using six or seven speeds.

Ideally, it should be done with the bottom bracket held in a vice, and with each side pulled out separately, using the controlled force of your bare hands. If a vice isn't available, then do it with one foot and a pair of hands working against each other. Make sure that the foot and the hands are in corresponding positions on each rear end, to get the best chance of an even result. In any case, you should always check with the "string test" afterwards.

You also have to remember that, because the

"Thumping" the chainstay

When a rider uses a larger-than-normal inner ring on a road bike, you occasionally have to do some "butchery" because the new ring touches the chainstay. This calls for some work with a plastic hammer, to dimple the stay at the point necessary to give the clearance required.

A similar process is often followed with track bikes, which have shorter bottom bracket axles, giving less tolerance between ring and chainstay. If a larger-than-normal ring is used, the plastic hammer comes into its own again.

Such "thumping" has never caused any damage to my knowledge, apart from the occasional lost flake of paint.

The wheels

The trueing stand

A good trueing stand is an investment. Of course, you can rough-true a wheel in a pair of forks, but for building wheels or trueing them properly you need a jig that can be attached to your workstand or clamped in a vice, and which has two points of reference. One reference point measures the lateral truth of the wheel, the other the concentricity of the wheel (i.e. its roundness).

You use a wheel dishing gauge to check that the rim is central to the locknuts either side of the hub.

Trueing wheels is not just a matter of having the spokes equally tight all the way round. Firstly, beware of over-tightening spokes, because they will just break. Secondly, build your wheel with its eventual purpose in mind.

All road wheels need a certain amount of spring in them, to cope with the various shocks of an

Two reference points on a trueing stand enable you to check the wheel for truth and roundness.

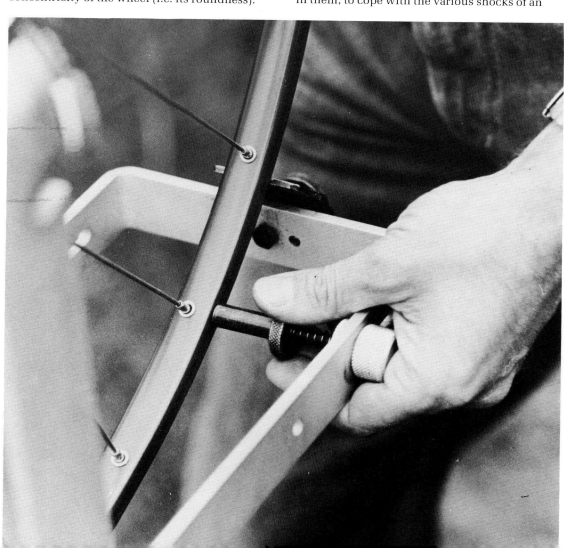

A wheel dishing tool checks that the rim is running centrally between the hub locknuts.

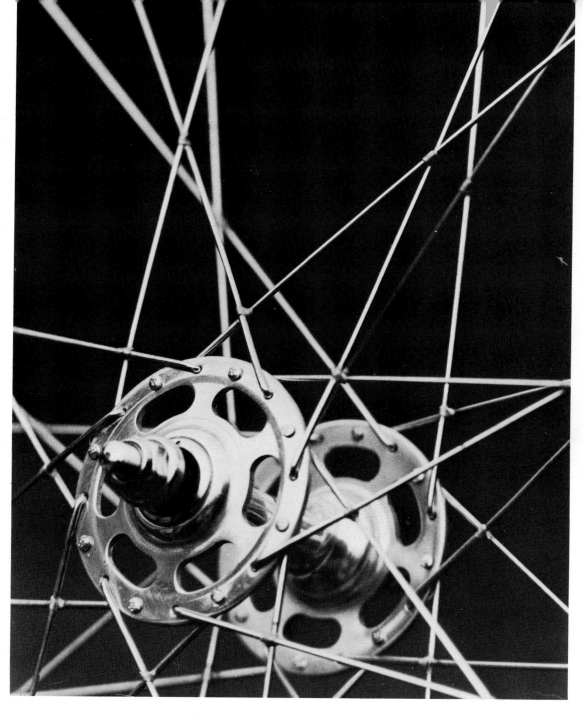

Double-tying and soldering a track wheel gives added rigidity. Note that the spokes are tied and soldered at both crossing points.

uneven surface. Six-day wheels, because of the extra G-forces involved, need to be as tight as possible, and should be double-tied and soldered to make them even more rigid. But even so, all wheels must have a certain amount of give in them. If you carry on tightening and tightening spokes, either they will start to pull the nipple through the rim, or else they will break — if not immediately, then after a short period of use.

Regular spoke breakages can be due to a

number of causes. Perhaps the rim is not true, and you are exerting uneven tension on certain spokes just to hold it straight; or the spoke-holes in the hub are too large or are badly worn, so that the heads are allowed to work about in the holes. Perhaps the flanges are too thin; or the distance is too great between the spoke-head and the bend, which allows too much movement at the hub. This is why you can get spoke breakages on the left-hand side of a back wheel, even though the tension is not as great as on the freewheel side, where you would expect more breakages.

The right wheel

At top level, wheels have to be built with the rider in mind — both his riding style and the event he is tackling. Weight doesn't have that much of an effect. But for tandem racing and indoor racing, the wheels have to be built more tightly, while the slackest of all wheels would be for cyclo-cross.

Large-flange or small?

For road use, small-flange hubs are a must. If a rider is sitting on a saddle for six or eight hours at a stretch, he will appreciate the extra spring that a small-flange hub gives to a wheel. For track use, large-flange are preferred, although small-flange hubs can be used for pursuiting.

Spoking

Because road surfaces are getting better all the time, 32 spokes are usually adequate for normal road use. For training, use 36 spokes, for time trialling 28 or 24 spokes. On the track, a sprinter or six-day rider would use 36, a pursuiter 28 or perhaps 24.

The rims

There are many different qualities, shapes and styles of rims to become familiar with, but I personally prefer the Mavic and Campagnolo ranges, which have something for every type of race.

In road racing, you have to consider the problems that arise when you swap from one type of rim to another. The angle of the braking surface, its width, depth, and even the diameter, will be slightly different; so the existing brake blocks will have to be changed and new ones fitted, otherwise you will have inefficient braking.

Another factor is the good matching of rim and tyre. You wouldn't try to fit a low-profile narrow tyre on to a Mavic Service des Courses rim, which is wide. It would look outrageous! Even worse would be a fat tyre on a narrow rim, where the adhesion would not be good enough and you would be inviting trouble. With narrow rims, stick to narrow tyres. And use narrow rims only for time trialling or pursuiting, because they are lighter and consequently not as robust as a road rim.

Occasionally you get problems with rims splitting at the spoke holes. This may be because the metal is hard and brittle, and there are no Longhi inserts to spread the pull of the spoke; conversely, the metal may be soft or the rim very light, when even with Longhi inserts you can pull so hard on a good spoke that the nipple pulls through. The danger signs are dimpling at the nipple.

With lightweight rims you have to be careful with spoke tension, because even with a quality hardened rim like a Mavic CX18, you can pull the nipple right through simply by over-tensioning.

It is easier to make a good wheel when the rim has Longhi inserts, because the spoke is pulling on the two surfaces of the rim, not just on the inner surface. But Longhi inserts do protrude on the rim bed. This makes no difference for a road wheel. But for a track wheel it does not make for smooth contact with the tyre; so you need to file down the inserts so that they are almost flush with the rim bed, before you start to build up a bed of shellac (see the section in Chapter 14 on **Preparing track wheels**).

All track rims should be corked, and the same applies to a light time-trial rim. This minimises the risk of a tyre puncturing from underneath when it's pumped up hard, as well as making it easier to stick on the tyre.

Hub bearings and adjustment

Most hubs these days still run on the simple cup-and-cone arrangement with which you will be familiar. Adjusting them is once again theoretically a matter of finding the point where there is no resistance to the rotation of the hub and there isn't any play either. And with track hubs this is just the kind of "feel" that you should adjust for. However, with road hubs, the action of tightening the quick-release mechanism actually squeezes the cones further on to the ball-bearings, so to begin with you need just the slightest amount of play.

Beware of how you use your two cone spanners. When you are adjusting cones, it is OK to use one spanner on one side of the hub as an anchor against the other side; but when you are actually tightening and loosening, then both cone spanners should be working on the same side, so you are treating both cones independently. Otherwise you risk weakening, twisting or even breaking the spindle.

Rear hub adjustment

You often need to make adjustments to a rear hub to compensate for a new freewheel arrangement.

Hub shells are the same whether the hub is to be used for five, six or seven speeds. But you cannot successfully use a five-speed hub with a standard six-speed freewheel or a compact seven. To change successfully you must have a longer spindle and a longer quick-release skewer.

The packing washers on the left-hand side are of a similar dimension, no matter whether the hub is for five, six or seven speeds, but the packing on the right of the hub increases accordingly. The measurement for a five-speed hub across the locknuts on the outside of the packing is 121 mm. For six speeds it is 126 mm and for seven speeds 127 mm. Because there is only a millimetre difference between six and seven speeds, you can adjust one to work on the other without changing spindles. Keep five different thicknesses of packing washers — thicker aluminium ones and thinner steel ones — to get the dimensions just right.

It is important that an equal amount of spindle should protrude either side of the locknuts, to give equal tension on the conical springs of the quick-release skewer, and for the wheel to go in easily.

So the procedure when changing to a new freewheel arrangement is this: first change to a new spindle; transfer the left-hand packing; put the correct amount of packing on the right-hand side; adjust the spindle so that an equal amount protrudes either side; then re-dish the wheel in whichever direction is necessary. The rim must always be central between the hub locknuts, otherwise it will not run in the middle of the chainstays or between the brake blocks. When you re-dish a wheel, remember to slacken spokes on one side before you tighten them on the other.

Changing spindles

You can change spindles without having to remove and replace the bearings. First remove the washer, lock-nut and cone from one side of the old spindle and fit it on to the new one. Then push out the old spindle with the new one, rotating it slightly if there is any resistance. It is important to exert some slight resisting pressure with the old spindle against the new one, so that they become, in effect, one double-length spindle, until the new one is in place. Then transfer the second set, with spacers where appropriate, adjust, and the job is complete.

Tubular tyres

Choosing road tyres

Picking the right kind of tyre for a given event is a matter of looking at the terrain, the road surface, the weather and to a certain extent the rider himself.

It is simple to say that a road race will need a mixed-tread tyre, a criterium a slightly lighter version, a time trial a silk ribbed tyre and a Paris–Roubaix a balloon tyre. But then you get the hybrids, like a time trial or a criterium on Paris–Roubaix roads. Then you need to take into account the number of bends, and whether the surfaces are good or patchy.

It is essential to get the right amount of packing between hub shell and locknuts. This is obtained using combinations of washers of various thicknesses.

Almost like magic — inserting a new spindle without having to remove and refit the bearings. The new one pushes out the old and takes its place.

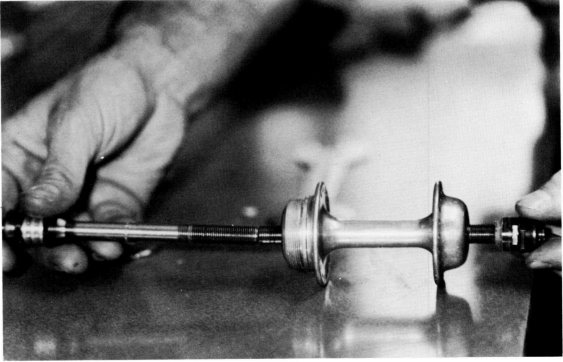

For general road racing you would have a Clement Criterium, or a Vittoria CX or CG. For a criterium you might use a Continental Sprinter or a Vittoria CX; for a time trial a Clement Nuovo Super Seta Extra, a Vittoria Cronometro Seta, or a Continental 175. For Paris–Roubaix you would have a Clement Paris–Roubaix, a Vittoria Pave, or a Continental Competition.

But watch out for circumstances which dictate a change in the "normal" tyre for the type of event.

Wired-on tyres

Wired-on tyres and rims are now increasingly popular for racing purposes, to the extent that some European professional teams are using them. The larger manufacturers such as Michelin and Continental have made significant improvements in their ranges to cater for this demand. The advantages over tubular tyres are that they are more convenient to fit and remove, and there is no risk of the tyre moving or rolling off, which can happen with tubular tyres when the constant braking on mountainous descents causes heat build-up to soften the rim cement. The disadvantages of wired-on tyres are that the rims will always be heavier for the same strength as an equivalent sprint rim and there will always be a sacrifice of 'liveliness' and handling, especially on bends.

Tyre pressures

Normally you pump all road tyres up to seven atmospheres (about 105 psi), which is the standard. Then you make concessions for the individual rider — letting out a little air for the light rider, or for one who is less of a bike-handler and needs more grip. Conversely, you put more air in for a heavy rider — perhaps 8, or 8.5 in the back tyre. This holds good for both silk and cotton tyres. The pressure in a wired-on tyre should generally be about one atmosphere less because of the tendency for the tyre to be lifted from the rim by the pressure on its tube.

You should go by the pressure gauge on your pump, because a silk tyre, for instance, will actually feel softer than a cotton tyre if you squeeze it, the material being more flexible.

You also need more air in a narrow tyre, and rather less in a fat tyre such as a Paris–Roubaix. Take this principle to the extreme, and you will note that a car tyre would need only a couple of atmospheres in it.

You can use silk tyres at almost any time in road racing, the notable exception being in mountain stages because of the safety factor. If a silk tyre punctures it explodes, and the rider could crash on a fast descent, whereas a cotton tyre will usually take time to go down.

Top riders will tend to use silk tyres for top events, such as classics or championships, but for general use cotton is preferred. Silk is lighter than cotton, but is far less robust, and so punctures and cuts more easily. And because a silk tyre is so much more fragile, you could be risking losing more time because of a puncture which forces you to stop than you would gain because of the weight-saving. A cotton tyre will puncture too, of course, but it will often allow you to ride on for a while until a quick wheel-change can be done at a more convenient place.

There used to be a philosophy that you didn't use silk tyres in the wet, but I personally have had no problems with this. All tyres now have a coating against the wet, so it shouldn't make any difference. However, silk does become more elastic in the wet, so it may feel softer.

Tubes for racing tyres are usually of latex, but being porous latex tubes lose air more quickly than butyl tubes. Clement got the best of both worlds by introducing a butylised latex tube, the tube having an inner coating of butyl which kept up the pressure while retaining the liveliness and puncture-resistance of latex. Continental did go over to butyl for cheapness and convenience, but studies have demonstrated what cyclists have long suspected — that latex is a more responsive material than butyl — so they have returned to latex despite its porosity.

Building up a coat of Clement rim cement on a road rim.

The tyre is inflated so that it starts to turn itself inside out, then coated with Wolber rim cement, or similar.

Sticking on road tyres

Sticking on road tyres doesn't need as much time as applying track tyres, but it does need method. First make sure you are properly equipped. China brushes from a handyman's store are ideal for applying the various cements. They should be trimmed to a point and to the right length.

It is advisable to put new tyres on to a rim beforehand to stretch them, so that when they are actually fitted to a racing wheel, it is not too tough a task. If your tyre isn't stretched enough, you will often have problems getting it on without getting some cement on the sidewalls, which doesn't look good. You should have stretched it first anyway, but once the damage is done you can clean it off with petrol. Petrol should also be used to keep your cement brushes clean.

When preparing the rim, the best rim cement to use is Clement rim cement. Build up a bed of three coats over 24 hours, then leave it to harden, preferably for three or four days.

Fitting the tyre, starting from the valve, and moving downwards each side, stretching the tyre progressively.

When you come to the tyre, you should first inflate it to six atmospheres to turn it inside out. The best cement here is Wolber or similar rim cement, which is clear, and doesn't show up badly if you have made a mistake and some of it trickles over the side. Once you have coated the base tape, then leave it overnight.

When you stick the tyre on, a mix of Clement and Wolber is good, as it has an ideal consistency and sticks very well. One coat of this mixture on the rim bed and the tyre goes straight on. Leave it overnight, and it will be ready to race on the next day.

It's worth noting that Clement is preferred for racing use because it forms a firm bond — very hard, almost like shellac — between tyre and rim. Dunlop rim cement always remains a little bit liquid, and in hot temperatures or on long descents it can start to run and allow the tyre to "creep".

For the same reason, Dunlop is better on winter bikes, because if you puncture you can change a tyre and still have quite good adhesion; whereas with Clement once the bond is broken, it is no longer effective because it is set hard.

Double-sided sticky tape specifically made for tubular tyres has become very popular, mainly because of its convenience over glue.

9 The transmission

Chain care

Running a worn chain is inviting disaster in the form of gears that jump or fail to mesh. And you can be sure that if your chain jumps, it will do so at the worst possible moment, in the middle of a sprint or as you try to respond to an attack on a hill. It just isn't worth taking the risk of that happening.

You should test for chain wear at the chain's most forward point, where it wraps around the front of the chainring. Pull the chain away from the ring as far as you can. If you can see the top of the chainring teeth, then the chain has to be changed, and scrapped.

Check the chain for wear at its most forward point on the chainring.

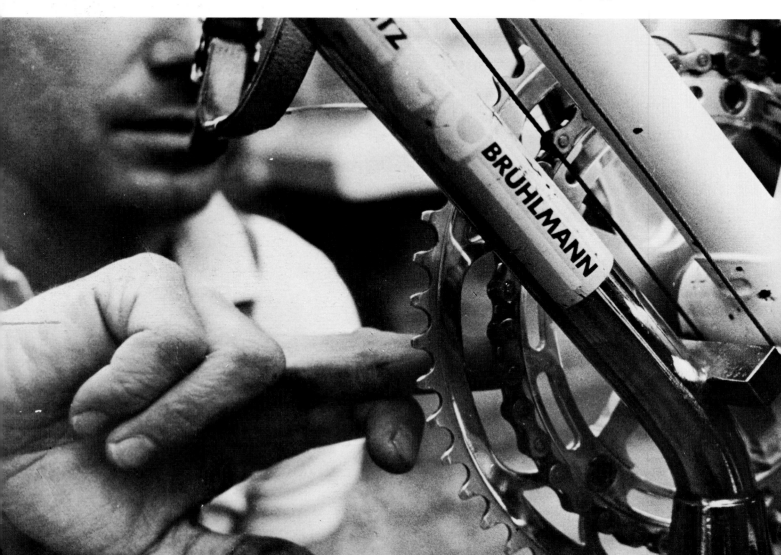

This means that you have to throw away the freewheel as well — or at least its sprockets — because a new chain will not run on an old, worn block. However, if you change your chain more frequently than necessary, it will probably run on the existing block.

Chain lubrication

Don't think that you must have a chain which is covered in oil or grease. Using diesel as part of your cleaning process will give the chain its basic lubrication anyway, and you usually end up wiping off a lot of excess oil from the outside of the chain, where it isn't needed. You only need

Often there is a pip on the outside of the outer chainring, to stop a derailed chain from falling between ring and crank arm.

Fit all chainwheel bolts loosely at first, as some may not be compatible.

oil between the inside of the link plates and the rollers, and on the rest of the inside of the plates where the chain meshes with the sprockets. And you only ever need a minimum of oil, since the more you use, the more dirt it will attract.

If you do have to oil a chain because of bad weather, then you should oil on the lower run of the chain so that any excess doesn't drop on the chainstays — only on the floor — and you should of course oil from the top.

I myself use three normal lubricants in looking after chains. During washing I use diesel, which

cleans and has some lubricant effect. Then for normal maintenance I use motor oil. For race conditions I use a spray lubricant such as LPS. In cyclo-cross I have even used spray anti-freeze to stop chains seizing up in slushy conditions.

Stiff links occasionally develop from lack of lubrication, which can be quickly remedied by use of oil or spray lubricant.

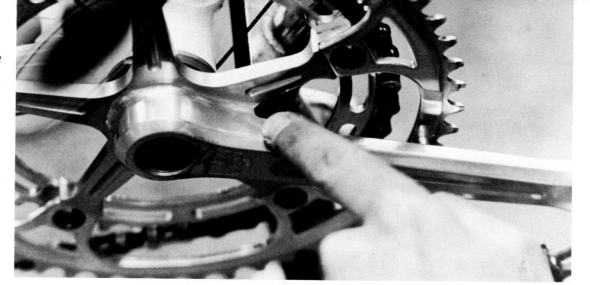

Sites of likely crank breakages: at the top of the crank arm, at its thinnest point towards the pedal eye, and across the eye itself.

The chainset

The chainrings

Fitting chainrings is a simple operation. You only have to remember to have the counter-bores for the chainring screws facing the right way, so that they face inwards on the inner ring and outwards on the outer ring. Also, there is often a pip on the outside of the outer ring, to stop the chain jamming between the crank and the crank arms if it ever overrides.

Having first greased the threads, you then fit all the chainring bolts — loosely at first, just in case there is any bad alignment of the screw-holes. Sometimes you will find that a nut and bolt just refuse to screw together, and you will then have to swap them over.

Another point to remember is that changing the chainring sizes, especially that of the large one, may affect the workings of the front changer.

Chainring wear is not a big factor. You should naturally change the ring if the teeth are hooked; but with good chain care, and regular new chains, the rings should last for a long time. Incidentally, old chains will run on new chainrings and vice versa, but a worn chain will make the ring wear more quickly.

Occasionally you have to deal with a buckled chainring or a bent tooth, which is invariably due to a crash. This requires a bit of butchery, but then it was caused by butchery in the first place. You can adjust it to a certain extent using a large screwdriver as a lever, or with pliers or some mole grips to straighten a bent tooth.

It must run straight again afterwards, of course, otherwise the ring is scrap. Again, if you have to bend the tooth too far back, it may be better to scrap it, as there is a risk of eventual breakage because the aluminium is brittle.

Cranks

It is a fact of racing life that cranks will sometimes break because of metal fatigue or a flaw in the metal. You can minimise the likelihood of this happening by frequent checks for cracks at the most likely fracture points. These are either near the top of the crank where the crank arms diverge from it, or about a third of the way along the crank

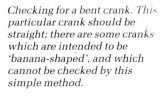

Checking for a bent crank. This particular crank should be straight; there are some cranks which are intended to be 'banana-shaped', and which cannot be checked by this simple method.

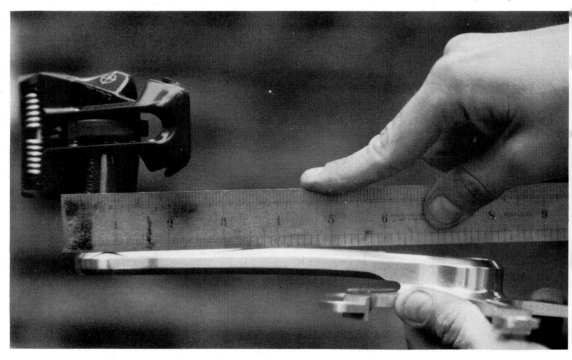

example, if the crank has been forced on too far, which is possible if you grease or oil the axle taper. Similarly, if you fit a pedal with an oversize thread, it can lead to a fracture across the crank eye because it is acting as a wedge.

The pedals

The advent of clipless pedals, and the new generation of shoes to fit them, has made it possible to achieve far greater precision in the position of the foot relative to the pedal, although it also means that such precision is far more critical: there is an increased risk of damage to the joints from incorrectly adjusted fittings.

There are various types of clipless pedals, some allowing lateral movement, others rigid; some capable of adjustment, others not. The most popular systems are Look and Time. Their great advantage from the rider's point of view is the absence of pressure points, an inherent problem with toe straps. From the maintenance point of view, clipless pedals have the advantages that there is far less to keep clean, far less to go wrong and therefore far less inspection necessary.

When you are fitting or removing pedals, remember that the right-hand pedal has a right-handed thread, and the left-hand pedal a left-handed thread. Always grease the pedal thread before fitting, to prevent binding and make it easier to remove.

Pedal damage

One far-reaching piece of crash damage which can be difficult to detect is a bent pedal spindle. The leg might become accustomed to it, but it can eventually cause knee trouble.

To check for this, you need a special pair of flywheels. They are made by Var Tools, but you might prefer to have them specially made. They are in fact threaded discs of extreme precision.

The procedure is this: remove the pedal from the crank, and screw on a special flywheel — the correct one for the right or left pedal. Hold the pedal on a firm surface, give the flywheel a spin, and if the axle is bent you will see that the flywheel is apparently buckled as it rotates.

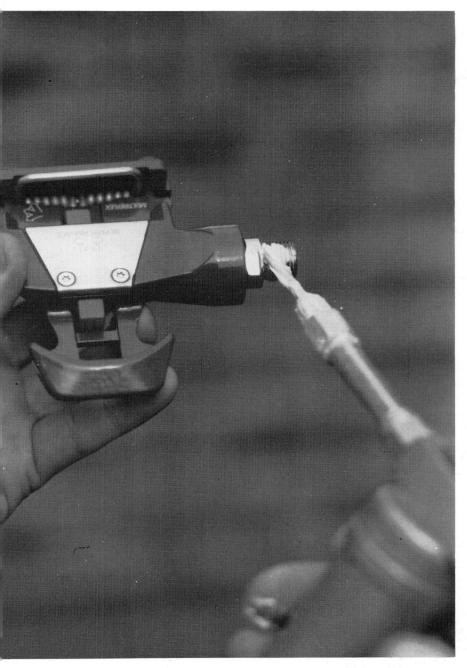

Grease pedal threads to allow a tight fit.

from the pedal end, or at various points across the pedal eye.

Don't expect your cranks to go on for ever. They harden with age and become brittle. Another cause of breakage is misuse in fitting — for

Pedal flywheels will betray a buckled spindle. Screw one on, then spin it: if there is a problem it will be magnified.

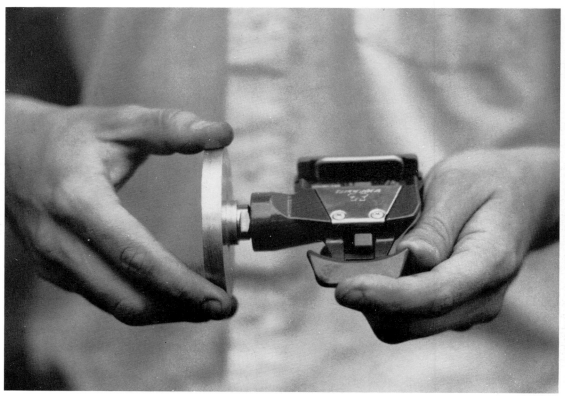

Toeclips and straps

Changing toestraps

When you have to change toestraps, you should take pains to ensure that the new ones are fitted in exactly the same position as the old ones.

The process starts before you remove the old strap. Mark the strap with a ballpoint at the place where it emerges from the pedal cage on the outside of the pedal. Now remove the strap. Set it alongside the new strap, and put a corresponding mark on the new strap, the same distance from the buckle. If the strap is to be used trimmed to length with an end-button, then trim it.

Now you can fit the strap so it will leave the buckle in exactly the right position. After you have fed the strap through the outer part of the

To replace a toestrap, first mark the old strap where it emerges from the pedal cage.

Put a corresponding mark on the new strap, and it is ready for fitting.

cage, give it one full twist. This acts as a security measure, especially if the holes in the pedal are slack on the strap.

There are a couple of other ways of fitting straps. One is to feed the strap through the slot in the backplate, twist it and feed it straight back out again. The other is to combine the two previous methods: in through the backplate and out via the side of the pedal cage.

The method you choose is a matter of personal preference, but involving the backplate does set the strap further back on the shoe at the side, which may be more comfortable for some riders.

Changing the method of fitting the strap will effectively alter the point on the strap into which the buckle serrations bite. So if the buckle starts to lose its grip, then you can extend the effective life of the strap by giving it an extra twist within the pedal cage, thus providing the serrations with a new area to bite on.

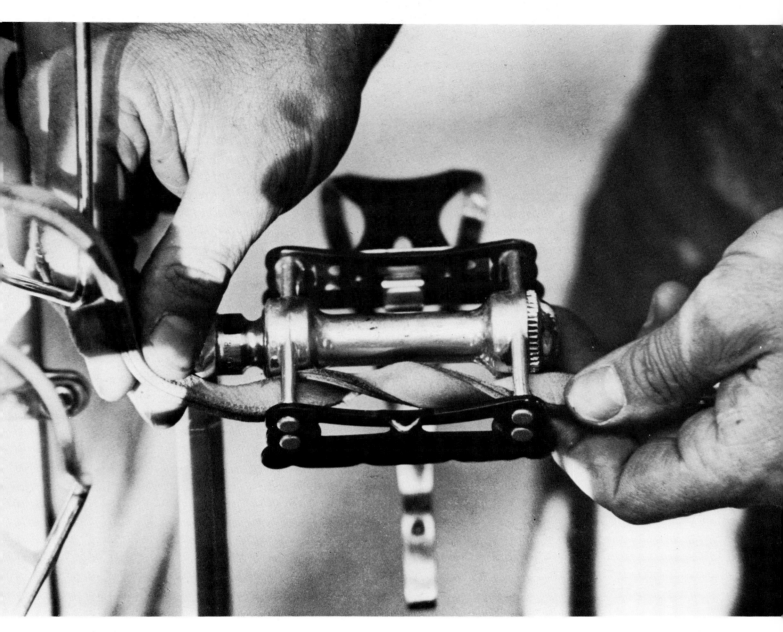

Toeclips

If you are changing toeclips, which is a
comparatively uncomplicated procedure, then
check the position of the old one before removal.
The purpose of the lateral adjustment on toeclips
is so that the front of the shoe is properly framed
by the front of the clip. Each rider's foot will find
its natural position on the pedal, and the clip
must be adjusted to that, not vice versa.

Sometimes the toeclip just functions as a carrier
for the toestrap, which then combines with the
shoeplate to hold the foot. But it can have a more
functional role if the foot is completely forward in
the clip, so that the shape of the clip at the front
stops any possibility of twisting at the toe.

101

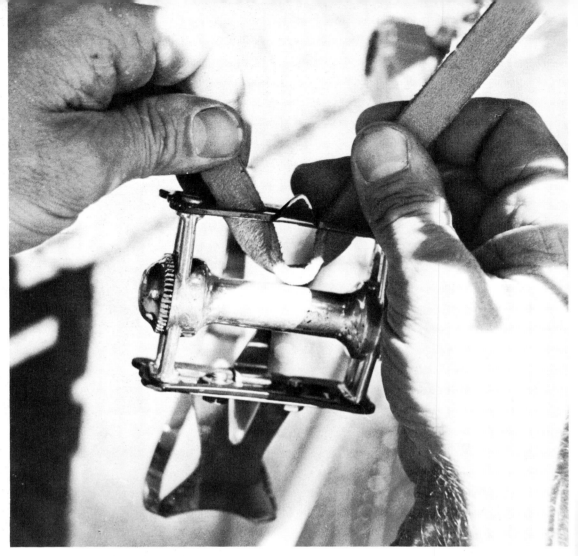

Two other methods of fitting toestraps.

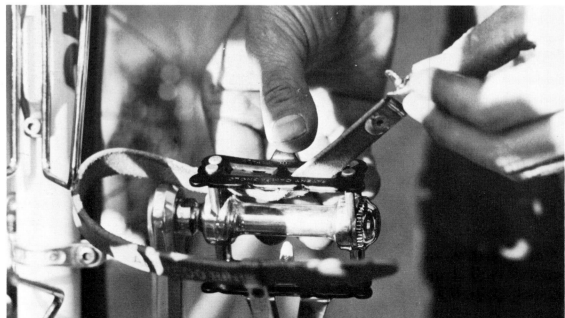

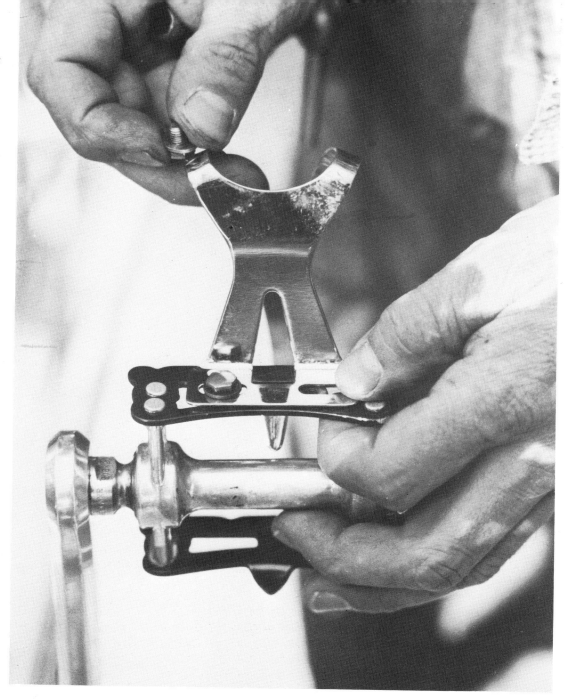

The positioning of the toeclip on the pedal is individual to the rider, and should be duplicated when a new one is fitted.

Nowadays, most riders prefer this latter method, despite the advice that most of us have heard to leave a gap between the toe and the front of the clip.

You can always alter a toeclip if it is not exactly right. Occasionally you have to pack out the clips with extra washers, because you want a length in between the established sizes. Often you will find that you get a more comfortable fit if you bend up the upper part of the toeclip so that it is more of a banana shape and the toestrap loop does not dig into the top of the foot.

10 Freewheels and gears

Freewheel maintenance

As a major part of your drive train, the freewheel needs to be well looked after.

It can be washed, just like the rest of the bike, with an occasional light oiling of the body from the outside, between its static portion and its rotating portion. Just a few drops of oil on a regular basis should keep it in good condition.

You need a light oil for the body — not the motor oil you would use on the chain. Oiling should also be your first resort if your freewheel starts making clattering noises. This will often do the trick, but if it doesn't, the body has clearly seen better days and needs to be changed.

Sprocket care

Since freewheels are expensive, you want to be able to keep them as long as you can. If you use a chain and freewheel together for a couple of months' frequent racing, they will have worn together to such an extent that if you change the chain you will have to change the freewheel sprockets too.

The answer is to change chains frequently — at least once a month at a professional level. This will keep the sprockets in good condition, and avoid your having to change them when you renew the chain. The mechanic of the Swiss Cilo-Aufina pro team used to change all the chains every fortnight. By doing this, he reckoned to be able to use a sprocket for four years.

Dirty chains also cause more wear on the sprockets because of the abrasive action of the grit, so keeping your chain clean will prolong the life of your sprockets.

Jumping chains

One of the reasons for a chain jumping on certain sprockets is incorrect spacing; another possible cause is sprocket damage. If, for instance, the 17 sprocket has become dished, or an incorrect spacer has been used, then the problem will often show up on the next-smallest sprocket, on which the chain won't sit properly, and jumping is the result.

If sprockets are worn, then the chain won't run properly and will jump under tension. You can usually see that there is no longer a symmetrical curve between the sprocket teeth.

Sprocket wear isn't always a slow process. Used with an old, badly worn chain, new sprockets can get badly hooked in only a couple of days.

Sprocket removal

For sprocket removal, a pair of rigid sprocket removers is quicker to use than the type of remover which uses a length of chain. The rigid type of sprocket wrench has a radiused channel at each end, which fits over the sprocket teeth. One end is used on sprockets with up to 21 teeth, the other from 21 upwards.

With the wheel positioned as if you are fitting a tyre, you must put one wrench on one of the largest sprockets, which acts as an anchor. The other one engages either on the smallest sprocket or, if the two smallest sprockets are connected, on the next smallest. Often the top sprocket screws into the next one, rather than on to the body itself, so you have to work on the larger one to remove both.

Using one wrench working against the other, you can easily loosen the top sprocket (or sprockets), and finally remove it (or them) by hand. Once the screwed sprockets are removed, the remaining splined sprockets come off without needing a tool.

Maillard freewheels are almost universally used in road racing, because their range is so

Rigid sprocket removers, used one in opposition to the other.

flexible. They work with the top two sprockets screwed and the rest on two splines. There are plenty of sprockets available, and they are reversible, so you can fit them either way and thus get double the wear out of them.

The Shimano cassette system is also good — a mechanic's dream, because there is only one spline and one holding sprocket. Campagnolo is also good, with two splines and one security sprocket, while the Regina and Sun Tour systems are known for having specially easy threads which don't bind up.

Get to know the various systems, especially where there are differing spacers, or where the sprockets can be fitted only one way round (as with Campagnolo), or where the splined sprockets are reversible (as with Maillard and Regina).

If you are using a freewheel with alloy sprockets, then extra care is needed. Here it is best to use a chain-type removal tool, which pulls on several sprocket teeth at a time, rather than the faster rigid chain wrench, which pulls on only one tooth and could thus damage a softer alloy sprocket.

The gears

Gear levers

Fitting levers with a fixing clamp is straight-forward, but the result doesn't look as neat as when you use braze-on fittings. If you are using braze-ons, make sure that the fixing boss is clear of paint, so that the lever can be fitted on flush, with the backplate fitting right against the frame.

With the modern system of bare cables, usually passing through guides under the bracket shell, there is hardly any need for greasing cables because there is very little contact to worry about. Similarly, if you use stainless steel cable casing for the loop from the chainstay stop to the rear derailleur, you again have no lubrication problems, and there is no difficulty with colour coordination.

Teflon-lined gear-cable casings don't work as well as the equivalent brake cables; but stainless

To give a more positive change, use pliers to pinch in the cage plates at the front.

Permitted butchery on a front changer: using a screwdriver blade to bulge out the rear parts of the cage.

steel inner cables are very good, and the plaited type is very much more flexible than the traditionally wound cable.

Once you have fitted the cable to the rear mechanism, slip a crimper over the end. Don't solder cable ends, which in any case isn't possible with stainless steel cables.

The front changer

Fitting or adjusting a front changer correctly is more complicated than it seems, because of modern designs. Whereas for years the cage plates were parallel and straight, now they are shaped to give better changing. In most cases you have to do some fine tuning to get the best possible change.

When a rider is pedalling hard it can cause the chainrings to deflect; thus what appears to run freely on a workstand might cause some chain fouling when under race pressure.

First of all, you must line up the cage so that its plates are parallel to the outside ring. Then you use a pair of pliers to pinch in slightly the front part of the cage plates. This ensures that the inside plate throws the chain more positively from the inside ring to the outside, while the pinched-in front of the outside cage plate acts as a control, preventing the chain from overshooting. Similarly, when you change down, the pinched-in front section acts to give a positive change, but without overshooting.

In the meantime, however, the chain still has to run on all sprockets without fouling the cage. Use the blade of a wide screwdriver, twisted sideways, to push the cage plates outwards on their rear section, and to give more clearance.

Most front changers need this kind of gentle persuasion to get the best out of them — although the job is easier when you are using a narrow chain, which doesn't need as much clearance.

This is another good reason for using a narrow chain, whatever the type of freewheel you choose. If you are on a narrow chain you can use any freewheel, whereas if you puncture when using a standard chain and freewheel, you will have trouble if you are given a spare wheel with a narrow block. Narrow chains also work better on short rear triangles — especially the Sedisport, which has a unique construction, making it extremely flexible.

The changer should be fitted so that the lower edge of the outside cage plate is about 2 mm from the top of the chainring teeth. Any more, and you don't get such a positive change.

The rear mechanism

Screwing the rear mechanism on to the gear hanger is simple enough. Just feed the cable through and pull it tight with your fingers or with pliers, and lock up the clamp bolt. Then work the

Correct positioning of the front changer is so that the outer cage plate just clears the top of the outer chainring teeth.

Having fitted the rear derailleur, trim off the cable and crimp the end neatly. Note the smooth bend in the stainless steel casing.

Deciding chain length. Running on the smallest sprocket and inside ring, the chain should just start to take up the derailleur tension.

lever a few times to stretch the cable and allow the short length of cable casing to contract. Now re-tension it once again. The stretch is immediate, so the procedure should not need to be repeated later, since the cable will already be fully stretched.

Once you've trimmed off the excess cable and fitted a crimped end, the next job is to fit the chain.

Fitting the chain

Install chains straight from their box, using the grease that manufacturers put on the chain before boxing it. In fact, the chain will run even more freely later on, when the grease has worn off a little and been replaced by oil; but for the time being the grease is sufficient.

Assuming that the front changer has already been fitted, you fit the chain first on the smallest chainring and the smallest sprocket, with the loose ends meeting on the bottom run of the chain.

*Chain rivet pliers are faster than
the conventional rivet extractor.*

*A stiff link, which will cause
chain jumping.*

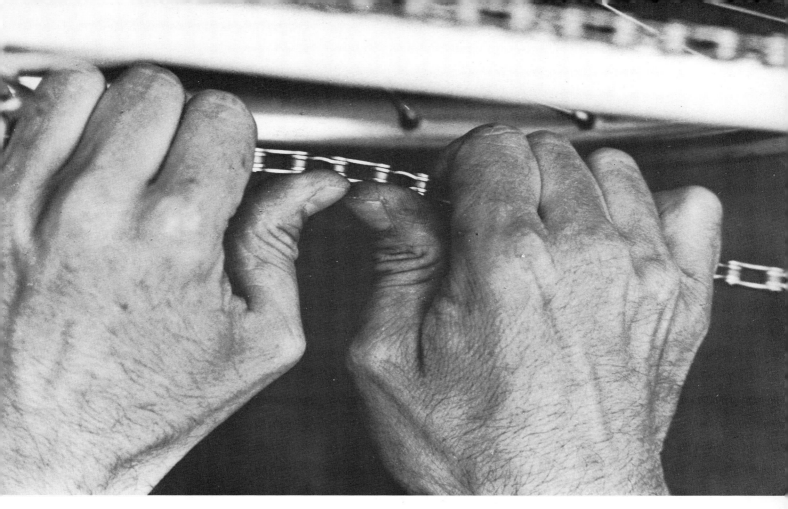

Tackling a stiff link by splaying it outwards using thumb pressure.

You pull the ends of the chain together, and overlap them until the spring tension of the derailleur starts to be taken up. This decides the length of the chain. The method creates quite a lot of resistance from the chain when the big sprocket and big ring are engaged, but it gives a much more positive gear change.

I have seen Russian teams that do it the opposite way round, so that the chain actually hangs down slack when it's on the small ring and small sprocket.

Chain pliers are better for the job than the conventional rivet extractor, and far quicker. You quickly get the hang of using them. I personally use Gian Robert pliers. Shorten the chain to the required length and then rivet up, using the pliers for both jobs.

When you are riveting the chain, try to ensure that the rivet protrudes a similar distance each side of the chain. This will ensure, not only that you don't have a stiff link, but also that the chain will run better and will change gear well.

With Sedis chains, which in other respects are the best chains, you often do get a stiff link. But then it is simply a matter of attempting to bend the chain sideways, pushing with both thumbs to splay the link out a little and thus free it.

With practice, you can use chain pliers so that you hardly ever get stiff links. The cyclo-type rivet extractor works well enough too, but it is nowhere near as fast.

With narrow chains, it is important that you don't leave rivets sticking out. Chains like the Sedisport, the Sun Tour Ultra, and the narrow Wippermann, are designed so that the rivets end up flush with the outer links. Leave the rivet protruding on one side, and you risk the chain fouling on a compact freewheel, or even breaking.

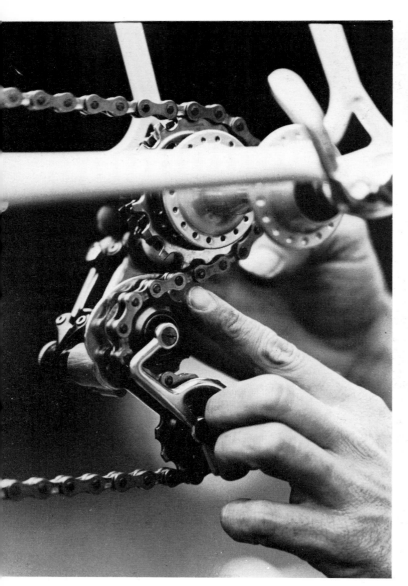

Watch for problems when you change to a larger bottom sprocket. Whereas (left) the chain normally runs unhindered between top jockey roller and largest sprocket, it can be trapped (right) if a larger sprocket is used. Sometimes moving the wheel back in the drop-outs will solve the problem, otherwise an extra link has to be fitted.

The method described can be used to determine the chain length for virtually all racing freewheels, even up to a 26 rear sprocket (which is fitted only in extreme conditions anyway). With a big rear sprocket, you may have to move the wheel back in the drop-outs so that the top roller of the gear mechanism won't foul the sprocket. With a 26-tooth sprocket you may occasionally have to put in an extra link. But most racing gears, no matter what their official specifications say, can be adjusted to handle up to a 26 sprocket.

The top roller needs to be close to the sprockets for a snappy change, but not so close that it risks trapping the chain in between roller and sprocket — in which case it either will not change at all or will change badly, and there will be a lot of noise.

Occasionally you get a problem with the smallest sprockets fouling the chain or seat stay.

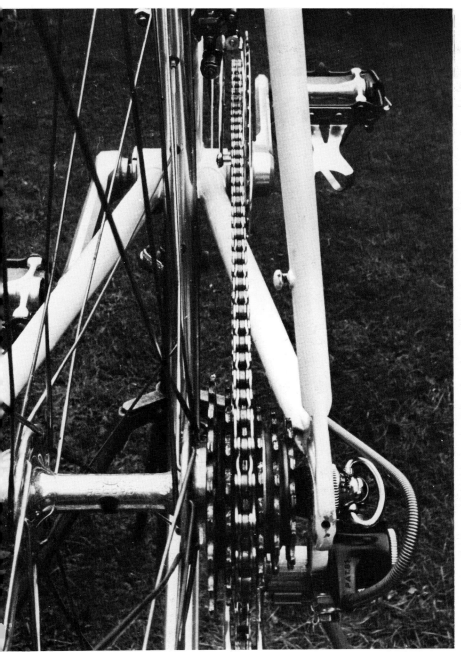

The chainline

To give your gears the best chance, your chainline must be correct. This means that the chain must be running in a straight line from the chainring to the most frequently-used sprockets. In practice, this means that the inner ring should line up with the third-largest sprocket, and the outer ring with the third-smallest, assuming you are using a six-speed block. On five or seven speeds, the centre sprocket should line up midway between the chainrings.

The above system holds good for road racing, where you are using each sprocket fairly frequently. In time trials, where you expect to be using the smaller sprockets predominantly, you shift the chainline towards the outside of the block, central to the most frequently-used sprocket. This is done by altering the spacing of the hub using washers and redishing the wheel accordingly (see the section in Chapter 8 on **Rear hub adjustment**). In cyclo-cross, where you are using the large sprockets much of the time, the chainline should move inwards.

If you are riding with a single chainring, have the chain tighter, so that the jockey cage is more erect, with less chain wrap-round. This will give a positive change, and will reduce the risk of the chain jumping off over rough roads when you change gear.

Good chainline. On a six-speed freewheel, the chain should run in a straight line between inner ring and third-largest freewheel sprocket.

Assuming the hub has been correctly spaced to begin with, you then have to use your file judiciously to give the sprocket room, bearing in mind that you can't file away all the brass or the drop-out will literally do just that!

The handlebars

Handlebar fitting

Fitting the handlebars to the stem should present no difficulty if you tackle the job correctly.

One major mistake is to mix the makes of bar and stem. For instance, Cinelli bars will not fit 3TTT stems, and vice versa, because they are of different diameters at the centre. So keep like with like.

There is no need to use anything to prise apart the handlebar clamp on the stem to insert the bars. If any force is required, then you just aren't doing the job correctly. Don't grease the bars either to make them fit more easily. The only time you need to lubricate is when the bars are

creaking once they are tight in the stem. Use LPS1, and this often cures this annoying noise.

Simply slide the bars into the stem, and rotate them as you come to the handlebar bend, which should avoid any resistance and stop them getting scratched. If you meet any resistance, just back off and try the bend at a different angle.

You don't have to put a lot of force into tightening the bars in the stem. If you are using a Cinelli 1R Record stem, which uses a wedge to clamp the bars, it can ovalise some of the lighter bars quite easily, so that they will never quite fit again. So with a Record stem, try to tighten the bars once only. Incidentally, you should always grease the threads of the handlebar clamp bolt.

The actual attitude of the bars is a matter of personal preference, but convention dictates that

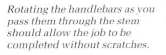

Rotating the handlebars as you pass them through the stem should allow the job to be completed without scratches.

Taking a sight from straight-edge to handlebar top tells you whether brake levers are at an even height.

This measurement ensures that the levers are positioned correctly for easy reach.

the angle of the bottom of the bars should be somewhere between parallel to the top tube and at right angles to the head tube.

The brake levers

Setting up the brake levers demands precision. Although some riders actually want one brake lever higher than the other, most will want them

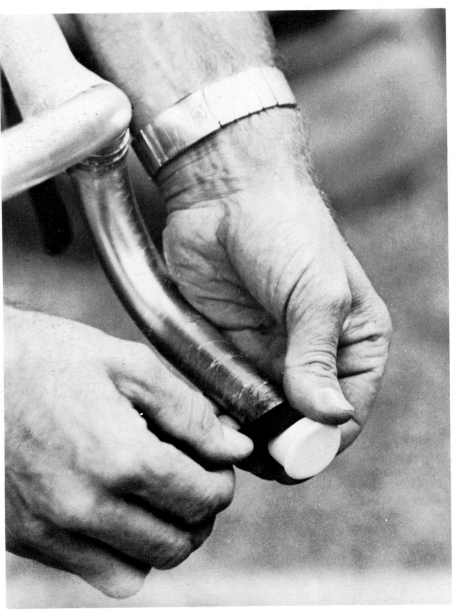

Before taping the bars, use insulating tape to secure the end stops.

level, otherwise they will suffer some small unwanted stresses in their shoulders.

Once you've set the brake levers so they are visually level, the best way to check their position is to place a straight-edge across the hoods between them, and take a sighting of the straight-edge against the top edge of the handlebars. This should easily show if the levers aren't level.

It is best to set the levers in position before you fit cables, since the very act of adjusting the tightness of the lever can damage a cable.

The other consideration about lever position is where on the bend you should site them. Riders have their own preferences, and you can use your straight-edge again to ensure the correct position: hold the edge against the underside of the lower part of the handlebars — the drops — and then measure how much the lever blade overlaps the straight-edge.

This only holds good, of course, if you are always working with the same model of handlebar. If the shape of a new model is different, then you must find the equivalent preferred position on the new shape.

The "correct" brake lever position must allow you to grasp the lever hoods, with your hand and wrist in a natural, unstressed position. And when you are riding on the drops, you should be able to reach the levers without difficulty.

Taping the handlebars

It is important with the handlebars to ensure that the end stop is not easily pulled out or off in a crash, or when the bike is dragged along a wall. Use a strip of insulating tape for this, winding it over the plug. Also, before you start taping, fold back the brake lever hood rubber.

Always start taping at the end of the bars, winding inwards. When you get to the brake lever clip, do a couple of loops over and under the lever before continuing to the handlebar ferrule or bulge. As you work, you need to overlap a little on the lower section of the bar. On the bends this should be about half the width of the tape. And always wind fairly tight. If the tape tends to be slippery, or if the rider's grip is such that he tends

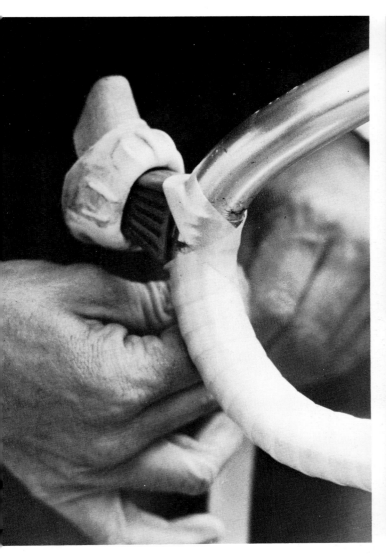
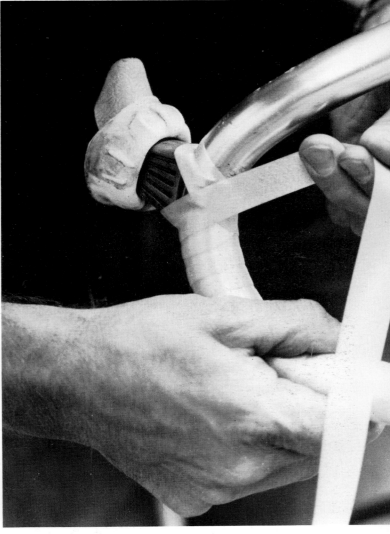

Two tape loops, one under and one over, cope with the brake lever.

to make the tape slide, then put a dab of glue on critical portions of the bars. This is, of course, only necessary with non-adhesive tape.

In fact most riders have turned for road racing to the Bike Ribbon type of tape, which has a thicker centre section with an adhesive backing. Cork Ribbon is also good, more comfortable and long-lasting. It is just a little harder to keep clean. Benotto handlebar tape comes in many attractive colours, but it is thin, and not as good in cold weather as the Bike Ribbon, where the thickness offers insulation from the cold bars. Cloth tape is

used much less now, and then mainly on the track, where it is changed regularly. It does, however, offer the best grip.

Once you get to the handlebar ferrule, use scissors to create a shallow point at the end of the tape, and then secure it with a trim of coloured adhesive insulating tape — a chance here to create your own individual colour-scheme.

You will notice in this picture that I tend to hold the front wheel between my knees to tape the bars, which seems to give the right kind of control.

Coloured insulating tape to secure the loose end allows an individual touch.

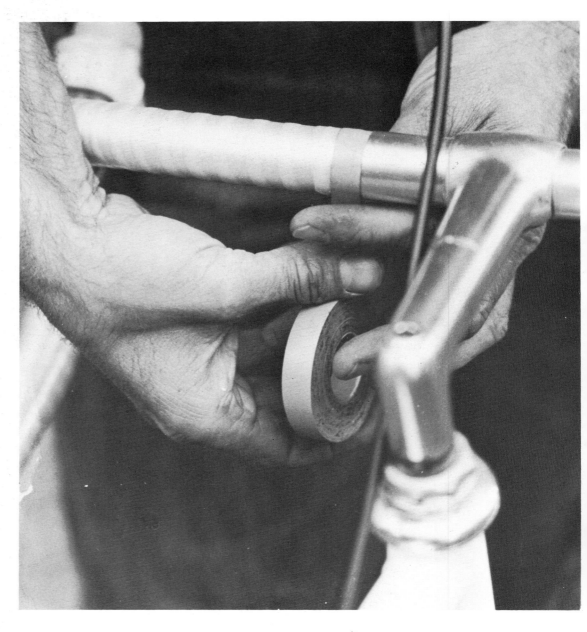

Bar butchery

When a rider has crashed and bent his bars, it is possible to pull them back into shape; but it should be done only once or twice, because the very act of reshaping them causes the metal to harden. In the end the manoeuvre will be very tough to carry out — and this is a sign that you should fit a new set of bars, or else risk the work-hardened pair snapping.

Drilling the handlebars for lightness is permissible if done below the level of the brake levers. On time-trial bikes, you can also drill one hole each side to allow concealed cables, but the exit holes should be drilled on the reinforced centre section of the bars.

Holding the front wheel between the knees gives good control when you are taping handlebars.

Saddle problems

The saddle is a very sensitive point of contact for the rider. If it is comfortable, he can get very attached to it — especially in six-day racing, where, because of the extra G-forces imposed by the tight bends, saddle soreness can quickly develop.

So a lot of chamois fat needs to be used, and this can sometimes work its way through the leather tops of nylon saddles, causing them to become unstuck. So one important job is to stick them on again.

Sometimes saddle frames break too. I usually carry spare Cinelli saddle frames for this purpose, cutting the old frame out and springing the new frame into place. It is cheaper to do it this way, and it preserves a comfortable saddle.

Some riders still use leather saddles in six-day racing, but the majority have moved over to nylon saddles with padding and leather tops, which need no "breaking in".

Occasionally, a rider has to carry on racing with a saddle boil, and to make his life a little more comfortable you can adapt his saddle. This is a matter of removing the leather top, scraping or cutting away the foam in the offending spot, and resticking the leather top. Occasionally you can get even better results by increasing the amount of foam everywhere except the area in contact with the boil.

Horst Schutz even had special saddles made for him with a series of bumps and pits to give him the most comfortable ride.

12   The brakes

The right depth

When you are specifying a frame, it's best to ask for one which provides a fair amount of clearance. The Piccolo depth brake, the shallower of the two standard racing depths, is adequate for most uses, and allows a fatter tyre to be fitted for, say, a Peace Race stage over cobbles or a Paris–Roubaix. If you cut clearances to a minimum, what happens in a race when you need a wheel-change and there is a fatter tyre? You just cannot fit it.

Let your frame-builder know the brakes which will be used on the frame, and the result should be that the brake, once fitted, has its blocks in the middle of their adjustment with the wheels you normally use.

If you have "fag-paper clearance", then you are at the mercy of a wheel which buckles, or of a bulge developing in the tyre.

Brake adjustment

Adjusting the brakes so that the brake blocks make contact simultaneously with the rim can be done quickly and easily using a cone spanner with the brakes applied. The spanner is used to alter the attitude "at rest" of the whole stirrup, so that the blocks will work at the same instant.

However, you may find this difficult with Campagnolo Super Record headsets, where the bottom race extends far enough out to stop you getting a good purchase on the adjusting nut. The answer is to put an extra washer in front of the fork crown to set the stirrup a little further forward, and thus give easier access for the spanner.

Using a cone spanner to centre the brake so that the blocks contact simultaneously.

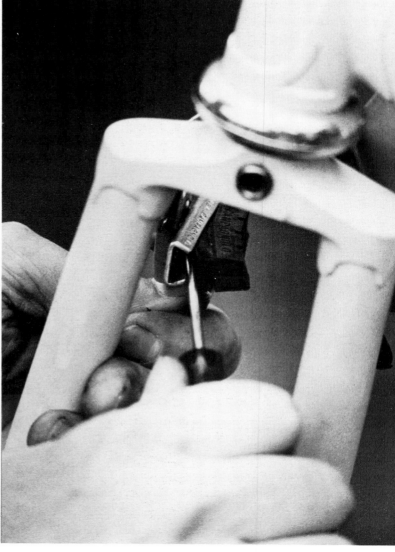

Centreing is more difficult with the Campagnolo Super Record headset, whose bottom race protrudes well forward. An extra washer in front of the fork crown will move the brake out enough to give cone spanner access.

Use a screwdriver to prise out worn brake blocks.

The brake blocks

Your brake blocks need to be in good condition, with the whole face of the block making good contact with the rim.

If they have been incorrectly fitted so that they develop a "shelf" where only part has made contact, this will not only give bad braking but will also hinder a good wheel-change — and you will have to change them. Also, if you are changing to rims which have a different cross-section, so that the braking surfaces are at a different angle to the original rim, then once again you will have to change blocks.

Use a small screwdriver to prise them out quickly and easily. Slide in the new blocks from the open end, having first "lubricated" them with a touch of soapy water or some good honest spit, which makes the job easier. Should the job get a little difficult towards the end, you can use some adjustable pipe grips to persuade the block where it has to go.

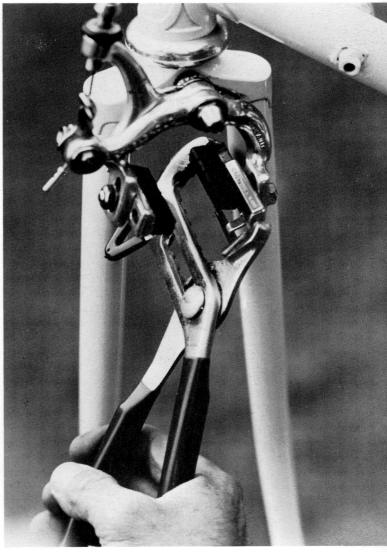

Slide in the new blocks from the open end, having lubricated them with soapy water or spit.

Adjustable pipe grips help to finish the job.

You often get brake blocks squealing. This is probably because the blocks are "heeling in", which means that the rear part of the block is making contact with the rim first. In fact, it is better to have the blocks "toed in", so that the front makes contact first. To correct the situation, use an adjustable spanner to give a slight and gentle twist (not a wrench!) to one or both brake arms, holding the arm just above the brake shoe so that the right kind of contact is made.

The only other reason for squealing is if some grit has become imbedded in the block and is scratching the rim, in which case you just prise out the offending particle.

Campagnolo brake blocks are of excellent quality because of the compound used, and they also fit many other brakes. It is also worth noting that Modolo blocks fit Shimano brakes.

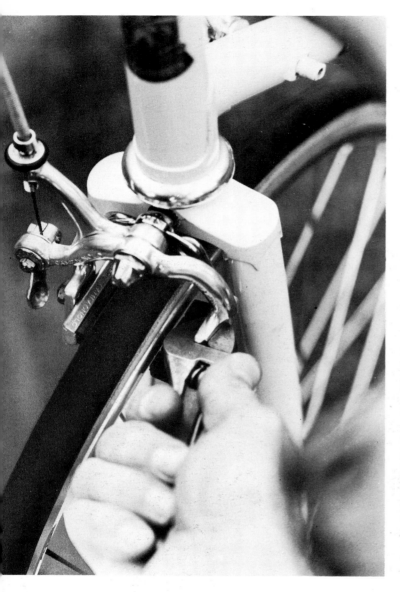
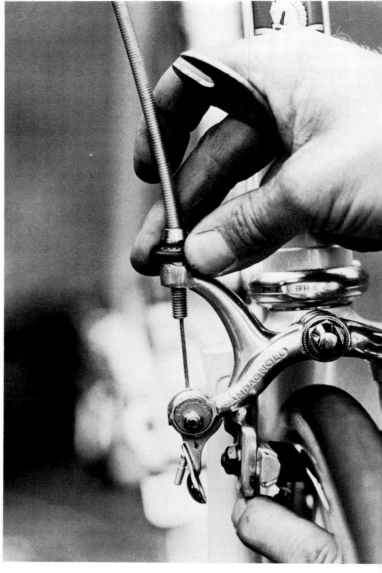

Twisting the stirrup arm at its lower extremity, to help the brake blocks to "toe in".

Start with the adjustment down on new brake blocks, so that it can be utilised gradually as the blocks wear.

Crash damage

Occasionally, in a crash where the front wheel and handlebars get turned violently, the brake stirrup ends up being bent as a result. As a temporary measure you can bend the stirrup back into position, but it is worth noting that all this manipulation can actually stretch the brake centre bolt, with the result that it needs retightening.

Cable adjustment

If you are fitting a new brake, or new blocks, fit them so that the cable adjuster is down — that is, so that you have all the tightening adjustment left to bring in the brake blocks as they wear.

13 My life as a professional mechanic

At work during the 1983
Rotterdam Six, giving
Hans-Henrik Oersted a good
starting shove.

*Crashes don't just involve
broken wheels and punctured
tyres. Often saddles, handlebars
and brake levers are twisted by
impact. Here two riders in the
Milan–San Remo are already
straightening themselves out as
help arrives.*

I never had the firm idea of becoming a professional mechanic; it was something which just gradually developed. I originally started systematically buying my own tools while I was still racing on the road and in cyclo-cross, simply because I wanted to be independent of bike shops. It was only after finishing a season as a professional cyclo-cross rider in 1979 that I decided to become a full-time mechanic. That was in 1980, the year that Tony Doyle became world professional pursuit champion.

From the time I had raced as a schoolboy, I had started to true my own wheels, and with some success. As a junior I had built my first pair of wheels. It had been a total disaster, incidentally, but I had gradually improved.

I had served my apprenticeship as a mechanical engineer, so I already had some idea of mechanics and the stresses involved in machinery. But my interest in cycle mechanics had developed really, not from my work as such, but from working on bikes. Anyone with basic common sense and a mechanical aptitude could have started out the same way.

Since 1975 I had had jobs with the Great Britain cycling teams. The British Cycling Federation had advertised in *Cycling* magazine for personnel — mechanics, masseurs and managers. So I had written to them, and they had offered me a job with a team in the Milk Race. I already had a decent tool kit by this time; so I just made sure I was prepared, with plenty of spare parts, and off I went.

The following year I was asked by Bob Thom to work with the Great Britain "A" team in the Milk Race, which was quite successful, Bill Nickson and Joe Waugh taking the first two places.

It went on from there, with more and more trips as an amateur, until in 1980 I decided I should be able to make mechanics a full-time career. It had already brought me quite a lot of travel, which I enjoyed, and it involved working on bikes, which I also enjoyed.

The turning-point was probably in September 1980, when I was actually paid as a mechanic in the Skol Six, a six-day bike race on an indoor track at Wembley.

In six-day races each rider is responsible for

Occasionally, in difficult circumstances, riders' machines have to be serviced from motor bikes. In this stage-race time trial, the rider is being shadowed by a motor bike on which the mechanic is carrying a spare machine.

employing his own support team of mechanic, masseur and a "boy" — a runner who does any job necessary. I was paid not just by one rider, but by several: Tony Doyle of Britain, Udo Hempel of Germany, Nigel Dean from Britain, Rene Savary of Switzerland, Horst Schutz of Germany and Kim Svendsen of Denmark. In fact, I had so many riders that I even had to employ a helper.

That was more riders than I would take on nowadays, but the Wembley event was at least fairly easy on equipment, except that because it was the opening event of the winter season all the wheels would start off needing a clean! I did eight sixes that winter, and eleven the following season.

The next major development came at the end of the 1981/82 winter season, when I had a message from the Swiss professional team Royal-Wrangler, asking me to go to their training camp in Spain. From then on it was into the big-time, with Paris–Nice, the Classics, and the big Tours.

The call from Royal-Wrangler came out of the blue, just because I had become known on the six-day scene as a reliable mechanic. It happened the same way when I was telephoned by the West German Federation in 1984, and in 1985 when the American 7-Eleven team wanted a mechanic for their European season.

The scene is completely different in Britain from elsewhere in Europe. Whereas in Britain even professional mechanics are sometimes expected to work for nothing by professional riders, in Europe even the amateurs expect to pay for your day's work.

Through working for amateur federations and professional teams, I have seen a lot of countries and done most of the world's major races: the world championships, the Olympics, the Peace Race, the Milk Race, Giro d'Italia, Tour de Romandie, Deutschlandrundfahrt, Paris–Nice, Tour de l'Avenir, Rheinlandpfalz, Tour des Flandres, Ghent–Wevelgem, Fleche Wallonne, Milan–San Remo, Tirreno–Adriatico, and so on.

Early in 1985 I had a call from the 7-Eleven's European manager, Richard Dejonckheere, to report to Belgium and go on the American team's six-week European tour. This meant starting with a whole new set of bikes, and working on 27 brand-new sets of wheels, including respacing the rear hubs from six- to seven-speed, re-tensioning them, and then preparing the rims for tyres. The brand-new Murray bikes hadn't even been seen by the riders!

Professional race mechanics isn't an easy career to get into. At the top there's a kind of elite. You can't get accepted until you are known, which means that you have a reputation that can be trusted. Imagine the disastrous consequences if a mechanic doesn't do his work properly!

And there aren't that many openings world-wide. I suppose every federation will need at least a couple of mechanics, but these may not be paid appointments. Every professional team needs one or two, and there are the mechanics on the six-day circuit, many of whom work for the pro teams during the road season.

I am the only full-time race mechanic from the UK, and I am probably the only one of those there has ever been.

I suppose I started to realise that I had been accepted when top riders and their mechanics began to ask me for help when they hadn't got the right equipment. And of course, when I was approached by the federation of West Germany — a country of engineers and mechanics — that was probably the biggest boost of all to the reputation I was building.

In my very first full-time year, I worked for Tony Doyle in his successful bid for the world pro pursuit championship. I was nervous, I must admit. I had to keep thinking about keeping calm and doing the job properly. If you think too much about the implications of making a mistake, then the nerves can get on top of you. As the pursuit event was progressing — race by race, step by step — I had to try to remember to do my job exactly as normal. Being systematic is part of being professional.

System is the key to the way I work. I have a system which involves doing things generally in the same order, but it is flexible to a degree. Not every job is the same.

If I have to break off in the middle of a job, then I have to be sure where to re-start again, so I try to stop in a position which will remind me where I stopped. For example, if I am working on a track

An experienced rider will do the maximum to help the service mechanic. This rider has stopped, removed his punctured front wheel, and is holding it above his head to give the mechanic advance warning of which wheel to replace.

If in doubt which wheel is punctured, an experienced race mechanic will run up with a pair of wheels to the stricken rider.

bike, and have to stop as I am putting the wheels in, I don't do the track nuts up by hand, because then it would be too easy to pick the bike up and think the job had been done. Instead, I leave the nuts extremely loose, or else tighten them up completely. And until I reach such a convenient cut-off point I do not allow myself to be interrupted.

When I started with the Royal-Wrangler team it was the first time I had worked with a European professional team, and I was scared — really nervous because I didn't know how things worked — and it was quite a long time before I settled down. But the very hectic nature of the European pro scene — always on the move, short of sleep — meant that I had to get used to it.

I remember my first Paris–Nice with Royal-Wrangler: after one stage we had a long way to travel, and then I had to work out in the street in the wet and cold, washing and checking all eight bikes, and having to try to sort out one that was badly damaged. By that time I was so tired that I hardly knew where I was, and a Swiss mechanic then helped me out to finish the bike, for which I was very grateful.

Because I work such long hours day after day, I tend to try to catch up on my rest in the service car, believe it or not! After the rush of getting the bikes in the car, off-loading them at the start, and pumping all the tyres up, as soon as the race actually starts the atmosphere becomes more relaxed. The team car rolls along nicely, and I become very sleepy all of a sudden. So I hold the spare wheels with one hand, the other rests on the door handle, and I just doze off.

The race radio is jabbering away all the time, but my ears are only attuned to the danger signals for me — listening for *caduta* in Italian, *Sturz* in German or *chute* in French, or for my own team to be announced. That is enough to pull me out of my doze, and I am suddenly awake and ready for action.

You will find that most professional mechanics catch up on their rest in this way, though not of course every day or all the time. Mechanics are an international lot, who appreciate each other's problems, and they will almost always help out another mechanic in trouble.

In the 1985 Peace Race, just before the start of a stage, one of the French riders found his gear lever return spring had packed up, so I simply went to my team car, pulled out a spare lever and offered it to the French mechanic — under the eyes of my manager and the French manager. He fitted the lever and replaced it after the finish.

In the Peace Race — the massive, tough annual amateur event which links the capitals of East Germany, Czechoslovakia and Poland — there is a code that everyone helps each other, and there is a competition with a daily prize for the mechanic who helps other teams. I won that prize four times in two appearances in the Peace Race.

Because mechanics spend so much time working side by side, friendships and alliances develop. Normally mechanics are self-sufficient, but one wouldn't hesitate to help another out.

It's not hectic all the time. Once I was with the Wrangler team in the Giro d'Italia; the race was very slow, and getting so boring that the manager and I decided to swap positions; so I climbed into the driving seat while he got in the back. After about 10 minutes he just nodded off. Then, just as the race tempo was hotting up, there was a call over the radio that one of our riders, Godi Schmutz, had punctured.

When we got to him it was a front-wheel puncture; I jumped out, and the manager handed me a wheel. I was in a bit of a panic; Godi could see that straight away, and told me to take it easy. I put the wheel in with the quick-release on the right-hand side — which on the front wheel doesn't make any difference at all. But it wasn't good enough for Godi, who said, "No, put it in the right way." It was *his* time he was losing, so I put it in the other way, and finally off he went. But it was a lesson that you don't have to panic.

On another occasion there was a big crash: I ran up the road with a pair of wheels in my hand, and found one of my riders jumping up and down in the road, with his bike at the roadside. It was a German-speaking Swiss rider, and he told me, "*Mein Rad ist kaputt!*"

Now in German *Rad* means a wheel, but it is also the short term for a bicycle (*Fahrrad*), in the same way that we shorten bicycle to bike. Thinking he meant his wheel was broken, I asked him in German, "Which *Rad*, front or back?", which just set him jumping up and down again, saying, "*Mein Rad ist kaputt!*" One reason he was jumping up and down was that one of his shoes was half off, and he was trying to get it back on.

Anyway, I found his bike and saw that both wheels were OK; but then I noticed his gears were bent, so I had to go back for a spare. By that time I had realised my mistake. It wasn't his wheel that was broken but his bicycle.

14 Track bikes

Track frames

People tend to dismiss the fact that there are different kinds of track racing, and as a result there are different kinds of track bikes, which each have their own characteristics.

A track frame will vary in design, depending on whether it is for straight-line riding (pursuiting), or for a burly sprinter, or for indoor racing on tight tracks. A sprinter's frame and one for indoor six-day racing will differ quite markedly, the sprint frame being much more upright.

For six-day racing the riders tend to adopt more of a road position, with the saddle well back. The frame itself must be very stiff. Weight-saving is not important. Forks, top and down tubes and chainstays must be very strong.

The sprinter's bike is very stiff too, but the seat tube is steeper, to bring the rider more over the front end. Because the rider needs to have a very low handlebar position, sometimes an underslung or sloping stem is used.

In the past you saw sprinters using a lot of steel accessories, especially bars and stems; but with good alloy this is no longer necessary, and steel components are nowadays hard to find.

The chainline

Chainline is very much more critical than on a road machine, and if the frame is correctly built for a standard rear track hub of 120 mm across locknut faces, then the line ought to be correct. This assumes that you have the correct length of bottom bracket axle, and that you are using the right cranks for the axle. Mixing chainwheel components can often cause problems here.

Naturally, you cannot afford to have the chain too slack. There must be some small degree of slackness, of course. To test it, just give the back wheel a flick to set the chain in motion, lay the flat of a spanner against the side of the chain and try to derail it. If the chain doesn't want to derail, then it's tight enough.

For sprinters and six-day racers, the 1/8 chain is almost universal, whereas pursuiters and points-race riders will find 3/32 adequate. In fact, in the UK and the USA, 3/32 is almost standard.

The hubs

You do hear tales of some track riders wanting to run their hubs without lubrication, but this is against all engineering principles. Danny Clark once heard a squeak coming from his rear hub and quickly dismounted. When I checked it, I found he had been running the hub dry, and it was so hot that the bearings were ruined. You need at least some oil in hubs, and preferably grease.

It's nice if someone picks up a wheel, gives the axle a spin and it turns for ever; but it's a different matter when those bearings have to carry the weight of the bike and the rider.

Large-flange hubs are best for sprinters and for indoor tracks. They give a more robust and rigid wheel, and consequently fewer spoke problems.

Only use chrome spokes on the track — not just for looks, but because there is less give in a chrome spoke than in a stainless steel one. They are double-tied and soldered.

Crank length and gearing

Gearing changes with conditions; but pursuiters like to get their gear ratio through using a large ring and a large sprocket, which runs more freely; while sprinters go for a small ring and a small sprocket, which they feel gives a more direct drive.

Cranks are usually 165 mm for sprinters and six-day riders, while most pursuiters go for 170 mm.

Authors Steve Snowling and the late Ken Evans look at an aerodynamic track machine.

The tyres

Tyre pressures

Pressures for normal track work are usually between 8 and 10 atmospheres. But the pressure you put in a track tyre depends on the rider's weight, the surface of the track, and the type of tread on the tyre. For instance, if you had a slippery track and a smooth tyre — which is a bad combination anyway — you would use a lower pressure to compensate. On winter tracks, using cotton tyres, you would inflate to between 10 and 12 atmospheres.

Choice of tyres

Cotton tyres are used exclusively in six-day racing. The wooden boards are soft, so you need a hard tyre to compensate, and cotton tyres are harder than silk. They are also safer, because silk tyres will explode on puncturing. Continental tyres — "Contis" — were once almost universal in the world of six-day racing, because they had so much grip and were very reliable. But Vittoria and Wolber are taking over to a certain degree, because they are good and — more to the point — they are available.

For hard tracks, the classic tyres have always been from Clement, although Vittoria and Wolber are also being used here too. Silk tyres are used more, because they are lighter, look good and sound better — all factors which can help a rider produce his best.

Choosing the wrong type of tread can cause problems on the track. On the Munich Olympic Velodrome, for example, which is an outdoor board track with a canopy, some British riders kept falling off, because the boards were slippery, and they had smooth-tread tyres in a situation where matt was needed for anything except pursuiting. On the other hand, Hans-Henrik Oersted, the crack Danish pursuiter who became world champion several times, was once riding an extremely grippy Vittoria tyre on the Zurich track, which is very rough anyway. The result was that you could hear the noise of the tyre against the track — not the singing that you associate with a silk tyre, but a rasping sound, which wasn't good at all. There was just too much grip. On the same track, Doyle was using smooth bands.

Pursuiters can use narrower tyres, which are faster, because there is less rolling resistance; and the reduced grip is not so important, because they are effectively only riding a straight line.

The so-called "white strips" are light silk or cotton tyres with a very thin, uncoloured tread. They must be used very sparingly indeed. On some tracks you will have to change them after every round or so. On Leicester, which is a very smooth track, you could possibly get through a pursuit series on them; but they would need to be carefully checked after every ride. There are several different grades of white-strip tyre, with a variety of weight pockets.

Preparing track wheels
Track tyres have to be stuck on so well that they will not normally come off when there is a puncture. This means painstaking preparation of the rim and the tyre, which is a process that cannot be rushed or skimped. The essential ingredient for sticking tyre to rim is shellac.

It is best to keep two separate pots of shellac: a thin mixture and a thick mixture. You make up the shellac mixtures by first buying shellac flakes from a chemist: you then mix it up, either with commercial methylated spirit, or with alcohol, which should be as pure as you can get it, perhaps up to 99 per cent. You should blend the flakes with the spirit or alcohol over a period of days, stirring the mixture regularly until it takes on a nice syrupy form. This you can use as your thick mixture. You can then take some of this and thin it down a bit more to make the thin solution, which is used to coat the tyre base tape. Shellac can be removed using methylated spirit, which should also be used to keep your cement brushes clean.

Preparing the rim
It is vital to prepare the rim properly.

With a new wheel, you must first cork the rim. You should have several different sizes of cork inserts to suit various types of rim, and fill up the spoke holes. Once the corks are in place, file them down flush with the bed of the rim using a Surform rasp.

Then the rim has to be keyed, using a spike or a screwdriver to gouge the bed of the rim and give a key for the shellac. Using the spike, score diagonal marks from one side of the rim bed to the other; then turn the wheel around and score diagonally in the other direction. Thus you end up with a series of diamond-shaped marks on the bed, which gives the shellac its key.

You should also use some spirit to ensure that the rim is very clean and free of grease.

Now start with the thin shellac, which should work its way into the grooves made by the spike. After one coat of this, you then apply, at daily intervals, a thin coat of the thick shellac — perhaps three or four coats in all.

You then have to wait at least two weeks — a month if you can afford the time — before sticking on the tyre. Because of this long delay, I always

Removing excess rubber solution from the base tape, using the back of a spanner.

Coating the base tape with shellac.

139

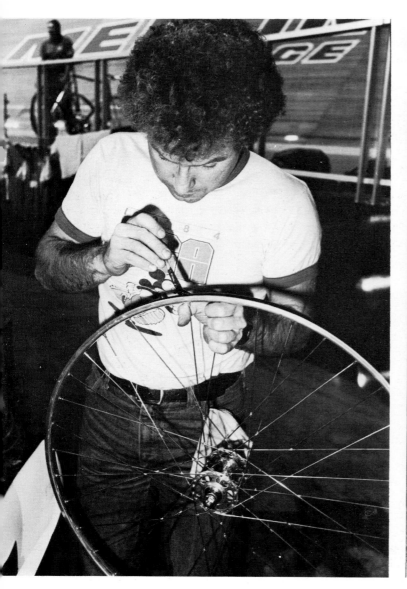

A final layer of shellac to the rim, and the tyre can be mounted.

Mounting the tyre.

have a few rims already prepared.

One way of checking that there is enough shellac on the rim once it is firm, is to fit a new tyre and pump it up hard, then remove it and see how much of an impression the tyre leaves. If you have 80 per cent contact, then that is enough, because the final coat will complete the job when you eventually stick on the tyre to be used.

This process of checking with a new tyre also shows you how well such a tyre is going to suit a given rim. Some tyres have a section which suits some rims well, while others will not give good contact. With experience you will get to know which tyres suit which rims.

When you remove the new tyre, no shellac will be taken off with it, providing there is no shellac on the base tape, which of course there should not be.

Preparing the tyre

The tyre should first have been stretched on a rim, to make it easier to fit. Before doing anything, make sure that there is no excess rubber solution on the base tape, left over from when the tape was stuck to the tyre. To do this, first pump up the tyre to 6 or 8 atmospheres until it turns itself inside out, and then rub the base tape very hard to remove any rubber solution, using the edge of a Campagnolo spanner or even a spoon.

Now coat the base tape of the tyre with the thin shellac solution, up to within 3 mm of each edge, since the tape is usually broader than the bed of the rim. This should then be left till it becomes almost dry, which means leaving it preferably overnight.

Fitting the tyre

To fit the tyre properly, you must first have put a coat of thin shellac on the base tape and left it overnight (or at least a couple of hours). Put a thin coat of the thick shellac on the previously prepared rim, and you are ready to fit the tyre straight away.

Now put in a little air — just enough to give the tyre some shape — insert the valve and fit the tyre, pushing down hard on each side as you go, and stretching it as you put it on. Put some more air into it; centre it; assure yourself that it runs in line, with no high spots, bumps or "egging"; then pump it up to full pressure.

The next step is to leave it in a warm, dry place. Boiler rooms are ideal. I've never known one yet that was too hot — though I do know of one unfortunate who put a wheel in a sauna, and all the shellac oozed everywhere!

For winter tracks, it's best to leave the tyre to dry for at least 36 hours, and preferably 48. For outdoor tracks, in summertime conditions, you can get away with it drying overnight.

Removing a tyre

When you take a tyre off, if the shellac bed on the rim has been done properly, it should remain intact. If chunks of the bed come off, then it wasn't done properly in the first place.

Instead of wrenching the tyre off sideways, first insert a screwdriver underneath it to break the seal. This should leave a perfect bed. Then all you need to do is to take a steel pan scourer to the bed to remove any loose flakes of shellac. And another tyre can be put on as before, with a thin coat of thick shellac on the rim and a coat of thin shellac on the base tape.

There are some alternatives to shellac, but you need to exercise great care. The 3M company make some glues which are extremely effective, but they only work with certain tyres. Something in them can actually start to dissolve the glue used to stick the base tape to the tyre pocket itself, which can obviously create big problems. So it's best to stick to shellac, which is tried and trusted.

Motor-paced riding

Because of the special stresses of motor-paced riding, the emphasis with the bike is on function, not looks. You often see handlebar tape that looks a hundred years old! There are also the brown bandages on the wheels, which don't make them quite so good-looking either. And because the wheels take that much longer to prepare, there don't tend to be a lot of these stayer wheels floating around.

You prepare stayer wheels just like ordinary track wheels — with shellac — but then you rough up the entire outside of the rim with some coarse emery cloth, to key it for sticking on the bandage. You have to allow plenty of time for the tyre to stick on to the rim, because once the bandage is on, the drying process is suspended. So you need a couple of months to prepare stayer wheels.

The bandage is the original cotton cloth which was used for hot-air balloons. It is about two inches wide, and two lengths of it are needed for each wheel. You stick it on the tyre, starting on either side from the outside of the tread, and going underneath the rim, where it overlaps the piece coming from the other side. There are small cut-outs for the spoke nipples. All this work is

*Motor-paced machines have
small front wheels and special
supports. Steve holds up Paul
Gerrard in a world
championship event.*

essential for safety: to stop the tyre rolling off if there is a puncture at high speed.

Because stayer tyres are fatter than normal, you pump them up to a maximum of 10 atmospheres, which is a lot harder than it would be on a narrower tyre.

Stayer bikes also have extra supports for the saddle and the handlebars, although the latter is no longer obligatory. There are also regulations concerning the overall length of saddles, which end up getting chopped off short, because the rules don't allow the front of the saddle to be in front of the bottom bracket line. So the rider finds his comfortable position and chops off the portion in front which isn't needed. Turbo saddles are easy to treat in this way.

15 Transferring the rider position

Measuring the angle of the saddle with the top tube.

Sometimes you have the job of transferring the rider position from one bike to another.

To do this job, start by assuming that the top tube is parallel to the ground, as it should be on all good frames (except those of special low-profile machines).

No two frames are exactly the same: they can vary in size, in length of tubes, and especially in the angle of the seat tube to the top tube. Even the height of the bottom bracket can have an effect on position. So to assume that two 23-inch frames would need the same amount of seat pin showing, or even the same stem length, is an over-simplification.

To do the transfer you need a metre rule, another shorter steel rule, and a measuring tape.

First of all, check to see whether the saddle is level or not. A good mechanic will know whether any of his riders likes to have his saddle away from the horizontal. Danny Clark, for instance, likes his saddle 3 mm higher at the front than at the back. Some like a slight drop. But the vast majority like their saddles level.

You check the saddle position in relation to the top tube, laying your metre rule along the top of the saddle, and using the shorter rule to measure vertically up from the top tube. Then you repeat the operation further along the top tube. If the saddle is level, then its height above the tube should be constant for its whole length.

Incidentally, for the job of adjusting the saddle, it's much easier to have a seat pin which operates from two bolts, so that you can just work on one bolt at a time to tilt the saddle. With the single-bolt pins, you find the saddle going forward and back at the same time as you are trying to tilt it.

You now know what saddle attitude you have to transfer to the second bike. The next step is to find the horizontal distance of the saddle behind the bottom bracket.

For this you first take your metre rule and place it vertically on the bottom bracket shell so that it touches the side of the top tube. Use a plumb-line to check that it is vertical. Now use your shorter rule to measure the horizontal distance from the peak of the saddle.

This presupposes that you will use similar saddles. If the saddles vary in length, then you make an adjustment. However, if the rider normally sits well to the front of the saddle, then you don't need to make any allowance for a different length.

Now measure the height of the front of the saddle. To do this, first lay a rule along the top of the saddle; then run your measuring tape from the top of the bracket shell to the peak of the saddle, and take the measurement at the point where it crosses the rule.

Note that this is not a vertical measurement, but a diagonal one from the bottom bracket to the front of the saddle, whose horizontal position you have already established. So if the saddle height is wrong and has to be adjusted, you will also have to readjust its horizontal position relative to the bracket.

With most saddles, when you move the saddle forward, you also decrease the saddle height — and vice versa. A 10-mm move forward or backward is equivalent to about 5 mm up or down. The one exception is the Turbo saddle, where because of its design the height stays constant when you move it back or forward.

The next step is to compare the handlebar heights. For this you take a measurement from the underside of the stem handlebar clamp down to the hub axle. This only works directly if the bottom bracket heights on both machines are the same. If they are different, then you add or subtract the difference. If the bracket is higher, then the handlebars will be higher by the same amount. So you will also need to measure the bracket heights on the machines involved. You can use a tape measure for this, though I have a special tool which is ideal for the job.

To check the reach, measure from the point of the saddle to the back of the tops of the handlebars. Remember again that if you alter the height of the handlebars, you also alter the reach, so you will need to adjust accordingly.

A cross-check on relative saddle and handlebar heights can be done using your two rules, measuring the height of the saddle top above the top tube, and then the height of the top of the stem above the top tube, thus establishing the difference between them.

*The distance of the saddle
behind the bottom bracket.*

146

The height of the saddle peak above the bracket.

Handlebar height.

Measuring bottom bracket height the conventional way...

...and the easy way, if you have the right tool.

Checking the relative handlebar
and saddle heights.

The reach: from the point of the saddle to the rear of the handlebars.

152

16 Equipment and parts I would recommend

As a mechanic, I appreciate having good material to work with, which is why this chapter has been included. In it I give some recommendations on equipment which I personally have found reliable. There may be other products which are of excellent quality, but which pose problems from a mechanic's point of view.

Frankly, I'm a Campagnolo fan. The quality is good — not always perfect, but always good to work with, and easy to strip down. Although it is expensive, you don't always need to go for the top range. One step down from the top range is still exceptionally good material for racing.

There is an international guarantee on Campagnolo material. If I see a Campag man on a race and I have some faulty components, I know he will change them. This is something which has become abused by some over the years, but it is certainly a worthwhile service.

Nowadays, components and groupsets from rival companies, such as Shimano and Sun Tour, are equally good. But now let's be more specific:

Rear gears

I recommend Campagnolo Record, although the more recent Shimano Dura-Ace models are very good, and the latest Sun Tour Superbe Pro is excellent, probably with better changing than any other gear on the market.

Front changers

Most tend to work well. I find Campagnolo, Sun Tour and Shimano all excellent, but they tend to need some cautious tweaking with a pair of grips to get the best change.

Brakes

Campagnolo brakes are of course very powerful, have very comfortable levers and are easy to work with. You can set the mechanism at various degrees of adjustment. Shimano and Sun Tour also offer extremely good models.

Handlebars and stems

Cinelli has always been my favourite, and is readily available. Cinelli make smart-looking stems which give few problems. The bars come in several useful shapes and in two or three widths. Good ranges are also available from 3TTT and Modolo.

Seat pillars

The best seat pillar of all time is the standard two-bolt Campagnolo, either the Gran Sport or the Record, followed by the Super Record. Many other models are similar to this design.

Chainsets

Again, Campagnolo are the best. You hear tell of breakages, but I have never had any problem unless a crank has been abused or incorrectly fitted in the first place. Don't forget that cranks have a limited life anyway, because they have to take a terrible pounding — being flexed and beaten and pushed and kicked and crashed. For me, Campag are still number one. Shimano and Sun Tour are also good.

Bottom brackets

I recommend the same makers as those of chainsets. I myself stick to Campagnolo, which last well enough, are easily stripped down, are interchangeable with other cranks, and are available in several axle lengths. There are a few sealed bottom brackets around, of which I have found Nadax a very good example.

Headsets

Again, I go for Campagnolo, Sun Tour and Shimano. But a headset is a sensitive thing, so be careful when you fit it at first. If it is badly fitted, or the frame isn't correctly finished, then the headset could be ruined within a couple of weeks.

Pedals

You can't beat the quality of a Campag pedal, although Sun Tour and Shimano are also excellently constructed. The best clipless pedal is Shimano's Look pedal; the Time system is also very good.

Saddles

These are a very personal matter, and come in many varieties of density, colour and covering. Good-quality saddles come from San Marco, Cinelli, Selle Royal, Sella Italia and Isca.

Toeclips

I have found nothing better than a Campagnolo toeclip, but it doesn't fit every pedal. Christophe have always been the brand leader and are quite good, but Campagnolo are better. They are slightly heavier; the chroming is good, and the clip is very strong. Campag's alloy clips are excellent too.

Toestraps

Binda have always been the market leaders, but only with their laminated models - Binda Extra for the track and Binda Super for the road. There are also some good straps from Bierreci.

Tape

This again is a personal thing. Good tapes are the original Bike Ribbon (often imitated), Benotto, and the good old Tressostar adhesive cotton tape.

Bottle cages

You can't beat a TA bottle cage. Other good models have recently come from America and Holland, but a steel TA (aluminium for time trialling) is unbeatable.

Gear levers

The best traditional system on the market is a Simplex with retrofriction arrangement, followed by Campagnolo. Excellent index systems are available from Shimano and Sun Tour, with provision for six- and seven-speed freewheels plus the traditional facility in the one lever.

Hubs

Again I prefer Campagnolo, for which spares are easily available. They are easily stripped down, and are lubricated either through the tiny holes at the side next to each cup, or through a centre lubrication hole covered by a dust cap. Shimano hubs are excellent, as is the Mavic sealed bearing model.

Rims

My first choice is always from the Mavic range –– the whole range, from the Service des Courses models for professional road use, to the models made for wired-on tyres. Lately, there have been some excellent models from Ambrosio and Campagnolo.

Tyres

There are some excellent tyres available from Continental, Clement, Vittoria and Wolber. Overall, though, the quality of tubular tyres is not what it was, and the performance gap between tubular tyres and the new wave of wired-on tyres has narrowed.

Spokes

Long-standing favourites of mine have been Berg spokes, which have never given me any problems; but Swiss-made DT spokes are even better; and there are some good Italian spokes. Another top make now is Hoshi from Japan — good, but twice as expensive as the best Swiss spokes.

Appendix

Gear table

Sprocket (Number of teeth) → / Chain wheel (Number of teeth) ↓	11	12	13	14	15	16	17	18	19	20	21	22	23	24	25	26	27	28	29	30	31	32	33	34	38
42	103.0	94.5	87.2	81.0	75.6	70.9	66.7	63.0	59.7	56.7	54.0	51.5	49.3	47.3	45.4	43.6	42.0	40.5	39.1	37.8	36.5	35.4	34.4	33.4	29.8
43	105.5	96.7	89.3	82.9	77.4	72.5	68.3	64.5	61.0	58.1	55.2	52.7	50.4	48.3	46.4	44.6	43.0	41.4	40.0	38.7	37.4	36.3	35.2	34.1	30.6
44	108.0	99.0	91.4	84.9	79.2	74.3	69.9	66.0	62.5	59.4	56.6	54.0	51.6	49.5	47.5	45.7	44.0	42.4	41.0	39.6	38.3	37.1	36.0	34.9	31.3
45	110.4	101.2	93.4	86.8	81.0	75.9	71.5	67.5	64.4	60.7	57.8	55.2	52.8	50.6	48.6	46.7	45.0	43.4	41.9	40.5	39.1	38.0	36.8	35.7	32.0
46	112.9	103.5	95.5	88.7	82.8	77.6	73.1	69.0	65.4	62.1	59.1	56.5	54.0	51.8	49.7	47.8	46.0	44.4	42.8	41.4	40.0	38.8	37.6	36.5	32.7
47	115.3	105.7	97.6	90.6	84.6	79.3	74.6	70.5	66.8	63.4	60.4	57.6	55.2	52.9	50.8	48.8	47.0	45.3	43.7	42.3	40.8	39.7	38.5	37.3	33.4
48	117.8	108.0	99.7	92.6	86.4	81.0	76.2	72.0	68.2	64.8	61.7	58.9	56.3	54.0	51.8	49.9	48.0	46.3	44.7	43.2	41.8	40.5	39.3	38.1	34.1
49	120.2	110.2	101.8	94.5	88.2	82.7	77.8	73.5	69.6	66.2	63.0	60.1	57.5	55.1	52.9	50.9	49.0	47.2	45.6	44.1	42.6	41.3	40.1	38.9	34.8
50	122.7	112.5	103.9	96.4	90.0	84.4	79.4	75.0	71.1	67.5	64.3	61.4	58.7	56.3	54.0	51.9	50.0	48.2	46.5	45.0	43.5	42.2	40.9	39.7	35.5
51	125.1	114.7	105.9	98.3	91.8	86.0	81.0	76.5	72.4	68.5	65.5	62.5	59.8	57.3	55.1	53.0	51.0	49.1	47.5	45.9	44.4	43.0	41.7	40.5	36.2
52	127.6	117.0	108.0	100.3	93.6	87.8	82.6	78.0	73.9	70.2	66.9	63.8	61.0	58.5	56.2	54.0	52.0	50.1	48.4	46.8	45.3	43.9	42.5	41.3	36.9
53	130.0	119.3	110.0	102.2	95.4	89.4	84.1	79.5	75.3	71.5	68.1	65.0	62.2	59.6	57.2	55.0	53.0	51.1	49.4	47.7	46.2	44.7	43.4	42.1	37.7
54	132.5	121.5	112.1	104.1	97.2	91.1	85.7	81.0	76.7	72.9	69.4	66.2	63.4	60.7	58.3	56.1	54.0	52.0	50.3	48.6	47.0	45.6	44.2	42.9	38.4
55	135.0	123.7	114.2	106.0	99.0	92.8	87.3	82.5	78.1	74.5	70.7	67.5	64.5	61.8	59.4	57.1	55.0	53.0	51.2	49.5	47.9	46.4	45.0	43.7	39.1
56	137.4	126.0	116.3	108.0	100.8	94.5	88.9	84.0	79.5	75.6	72.0	68.7	65.7	63.0	60.4	58.1	56.0	54.0	52.1	50.4	48.7	47.3	45.8	44.5	39.8
57	139.9	128.2	118.3	109.9	102.6	96.1	90.5	85.5	81.0	76.9	73.3	69.9	66.9	64.1	61.6	59.2	57.0	54.9	53.1	51.3	49.6	48.1	46.6	45.3	40.5
58	142.3	130.5	120.4	111.9	104.4	97.6	92.1	87.0	82.4	78.3	74.6	71.2	68.0	65.3	62.7	60.2	58.0	55.9	54.0	52.2	50.5	48.9	47.5	46.1	41.2
59	144.8	132.7	122.5	113.8	106.2	99.6	93.7	88.5	83.6	79.6	75.8	72.4	69.3	66.3	63.7	61.2	59.0	56.9	54.9	53.1	51.3	49.8	48.3	46.9	41.9
60	147.2	135.0	124.6	115.7	108.0	101.2	95.3	90.0	85.3	81.0	77.1	73.6	70.4	67.5	64.8	62.3	60.0	57.8	55.8	54.0	52.2	50.6	49.1	47.6	42.6

157

Index